PLEASE RETURN THIS ITEM
BY THE DUE DATE TO ANY
TULSA CITY-COUNTY LIBRARY.

FINES ARE 5¢ PER DAY; A
MAXIMUM OF $1.00 PER ITEM.

811.52 E24i 1976
  Edson, Russell
    Intuitive journey and other works

4/77

TULSA CITY-COUNTY LIBRARY SYSTEM
Tulsa, Oklahoma

Any resident of Tulsa County may bor-
row books.

A fine must be paid for each book kept
overtime (Sundays and holidays in-
cluded).

Books may be returned to any library
agency in Tulsa County.

The Intuitive Journey and Other Works

Also by Russell Edson

THE FALLING SICKNESS: FOUR PLAYS (*New Directions, 1975*)
THE CLAM THEATRE (*Wesleyan University Press, 1973*)
THE CHILDHOOD OF AN EQUESTRIAN (*Harper & Row, 1973*)
WHAT A MAN CAN SEE (*The Jargon Society, 1969*)
THE VERY THING THAT HAPPENS, *Introduction by Denise Levertov.*
(*New Directions, 1964*)

The Intuitive Journey
and Other Works

RUSSELL EDSON

Harper & Row, Publishers

NEW YORK, HAGERSTOWN, SAN FRANCISCO, LONDON

This book includes, in somewhat different arrangement, the contents of *The Childhood of an Equestrian,* published by Harper & Row in 1973, copyright © 1973 by Russell Edson.

Acknowledgment is made for permission to reprint the following:
"Catastrophe at Sea," "The Neighborhood Dog," first published in *The Agni Review.*
"The Ascension of the Cow," "The Gingerbread Woman," "In Here," "The Pipe Smokers," first published in *The American Poetry Review.*
"A New Life," "The Traveler," "When the God Returns," "The Youngster," first published in *Arion's Dolphin.*
"One Who Journeys in a Tree," "The Overlap of Worlds," first published in *The Beloit Poetry Journal* (a chapbook for David Ignatow).
"The Pilot," first published in *Broadway Boogie.*
"The Hand Squeezing," "In the Forest," first published in *Field.*
"The Little Lady," "The Terrible Angel," first published in *Hard Pressed.*
"The House of Clyde Bricabrac," "How Things are Turning Out," first published in *Ironwood.*
"House Building," first published in *Lemming.*
"Far From the Bureaucracy of Heaven," first published in *Living Hand.*
"The Incredible Accident," first published in *Madrona.*
"The Canoeing," first published in *Next.*
"The Abyss," "The Cook's Consent," "The Dog," "The Judgment," "The Song of Dr. Brilliantine," first published in *Occurrence.*

(CONTINUED)

THE INTUITIVE JOURNEY AND OTHER WORKS. Copyright © 1976 by Russell Edson. All rights reserved. Printed in the United States of America. No part of this book may be used or reproduced in any manner whatsoever without written permission except in the case of brief quotations embodied in critical articles and reviews: For information address Harper & Row, Publishers, Inc., 10 East 53rd Street, New York, N.Y. 10022. Published simultaneously in Canada by Fitzhenry & Whiteside Limited, Toronto.

FIRST EDITION

Designed by C. Linda Dingler

Library of Congress Cataloging in Publication Data

Edson, Russell.
  The intuitive journey and other works.
  I. Title.
PS3509.D583A17   1976   811'.5'2   75–30331
ISBN 0–06–011118–6
ISBN 0–06–011121–6 pbk.

76 77 78 79 80 10 9 8 7 6 5 4 3 2 1

811.52
E24i
1976

"A Brother's Description/A Night Song," "The Gentlemen in the Meadow" (under the title "Men Floating in the Meadow"), first published in *The Ohio Review.*

"Nothing" first published in *Pebble.*

"Another Appointment," "Baloney," "The Explosion at the Club," "The Feet of the Fat Man," "The Great Journey Blocked by Breakfast," "Mr. & Mrs. Duck Dinner," "The Old Woman's Breakfast," first published in *Poetry Now.*

"The Intuitive Journey," first published in *Seneca Review.*

"The Marionettes of Distant Masters," first published in *Skywriting.*

"The Dog's Dinner," first published in *Three Rivers Poetry Journal.*

"The Fisherman, or When Things Go Amiss," first published by *The Tribal Press* in their *The One-Page Novel* series.

"Dr. Nigel Bruce Watson Counting," first published in *TriQuarterly.*

"The Hemorrhoid Epidemic" was included in *Poetry in Public Places,* N.Y.C.

"Counting Sheep" was included in the anthology *Ask the Poet: Fifty Contemporary Poems Analysed by Their Authors,* edited by Alberta T. Turner, and published by David McKay Co., Inc.

TULSA CITY-COUNTY LIBRARY

For Frances

CONTENTS

THE INTUITIVE JOURNEY

Far from the Bureaucracy of Heaven

A New Life

The Intuitive Journey

The CHILDHOOD OF AN EQUESTRIAN

The Childhood of an Equestrian

A Journey Through the Moonlight

A Performance at Hog Theater

xi

The Toy-Maker

I am grateful to the Guggenheim Founda-
tion, who supported me generously while I
wrote this book.

R. E.

THE INTUITIVE JOURNEY

Far from the Bureaucracy of Heaven

The House of Clyde Bricabrac

He finds a how to build yourself a house plan in the street. He writes home to his mother telling her of his good fortune, of how he had picked up a piece of paper in the street to use between his teeth, and then noticed the instructions printed on it, CLYDE BRICABRAC'S BUILD YOURSELF A HOUSE PLAN.

In the left-hand corner, in small print, it tells how Clyde Bricabrac began as a shiftless man who used to suck his teeth and smoke cigarettes, and how he never went to good movies, and wasted his time drinking Cokes all the time, and didn't get no exercise, and was always cracking his knuckles so that no nice girls would dance with him . . . Then one day Clyde Bricabrac, looking for a piece of paper to use between his teeth, found a build yourself a house plan in the street, and how he then stopped sucking his teeth, and used a gold toothpick in the bathroom, and went to movies; also, how he stopped drinking Cokes all the time and started drinking orangeades, and was dancing all the time now with nice girls for having stopped cracking his knuckles . . .

His mother writes back, Dear Clyde, do be careful about picking things up in the street, particularly paper when it's to be used in your mouth to dislodge unwanted materials between your teeth. It is possible to mistakenly pick up money. There is nothing dirtier than money, particularly when used to dislodge unwanted materials adhering between the teeth.

Keep up the good work. I do really believe that one day you will take your rightful place on the dance floor with nice girls. Your knuckle cracking, while most certainly ill-advised, is not necessarily unhygienic . . .

The Terrible Angel

In a nursery a mother can't get her baby out of its cradle. The baby, it has turned to wood, it has become part of its own cradle.

The mother, she cries, tilting, one foot raised, as if in flight for the front door, just hearing her husband's car in the driveway; but can't, the carpet holds her . . .

Her husband, he hears her, he wants to rush to her, but can't, the door of the car won't open . . .

The wife, she no longer calls, she has been taken into the carpet, and is part of it; a piece of carpet in the shape of a woman tilted, one foot raised as if to flight.

The husband, he no longer struggles toward his wife. As if he sleeps he has been drawn into the seat of his car; a man sculptured in upholstery.

In the nursery the wooden baby stares with wooden eyes into the last red of the setting sun, even as the darkness that forms in the east begins to join the shadows of the house; the darkness that rises out of the cellar, seeping out from under furniture, oozing from the cracks in the floor . . . The shadow that suddenly collects in the corner of the nursery like the presence of something that was always there . . .

The Cook's Consent, or The Roof Episode

A kitchen explodes and throws the Cook up on the roof.

When the Cook comes awake the Cook says, why do I want to be up here?

The Cook answers, because I have to be someplace, haven't I?

But, why up here?

The Cook answers, but, why not up here?

The Cook's mistress, who has been having lemonade with her dog, Falstaff, in the garden, sees the Cook on the roof, and calls up, Cook, why do you want to be up there?

Because I have to be someplace, haven't I?

Yes, but, why up there? says the Cook's mistress, you're not cooking the roof for dinner, are you?

Why not up here, I have to be someplace, haven't I?

You're not making shingle soup, are you? Perhaps you're making gutter stew. I never heard of gutter stew. I imagine it's very tasty. Perhaps you're planning to roast the chimney? Is that a good dish? Or is it weather vane salad? Perhaps you'll surprise us with some attic window pudding? Or is it grilled television antenna? Do make up your mind, Cook, I am growing out of patience with your roof episode.

The Cook says, why do I want to be up here? Is being up here the same as wanting to be up here?

Oh, don't say that, Cook, don't make it as if I put it that way, says the Cook's mistress.

But, why here?

But, why not up there, says the Cook's mistress, you have, after all, to be someplace, haven't you? . . . Perhaps you might even incorporate some of those clouds up there in one of your dessert recipes; I should think they make a marvelous meringue . . .

But, Mistress, says the Cook, is being up here the same as wanting to be up here? I mean, just because we don't commit suicide, is that reason to believe we give our consent to be born?

Oh, do make up your mind, Cook, I am growing out of patience with your roof episode!

I didn't ask to be born—but it's okay, I give my consent.

A little late, but at least that's decided, said the Cook's mistress.

How Things Are Turning Out

FOR MICHAEL CUDDIHY

A man registers some pigeons at a hotel. They fly up to their rooms. He's not sure that his mind doesn't fly with them . . .

He asks the desk clerk if everything seems all right. He would like to know if the smoke coming out of his cigarette is real, or something the management has had painted on the wall?

The desk clerk has turned his back and is sorting the mail.

Sir . . . , says the man.

But the desk clerk continues to arrange the mail.

Sir, would you look this way for a moment?

I can hear you, I'm just sorting the mail.

I wanted you to notice the smoke of my cigarette . . . Since the pigeons flew up to their rooms . . . You never know about the future, I mean how things will finally turn out . . . Please, could you check my smoke . . . ?

When the desk clerk turns his face is covered with hair, like the back of his head; and the front of his body is like the back of his body.

Where is your front?

My twin brother has the fronts; I was born with two backs . . . I always got the spankings . . . But why regret the past?

That's good philosophy . . .

My best subject.

. . . Tell me, is everything turning out all right?

So far so good . . .

The Monkey Beaters

After several nights of beating a monkey they take it up the mountains to a hotel, and check it in as simply someone with a bad case of hair, and too nervous to shave.

Our friend, the one with the bad case of hair, that is, of course, if it's all right with the management, will rest here, in this resort location, drinking highballs . . .

The monkey is taken upstairs to the honeymoon suite.

. . . The view of the mountains and valley is particularly beautiful this time of year. And the balcony is a particular pleasure, that is, for viewing the mountains and valley, which are particularly beautiful this time of year . . .

After the bellhops leave they continue beating the monkey.

After a while they tell the hotel manager that their friend, the one with the bad case of hair, doesn't find the altitude high enough, even for the lovely views, the mountains and valley and all, and excellent service. Their friend, the one with the bad case of hair, has decided to spend the rest of his vacation in a balloon.

At the airdrome the monkey is passed off as simply someone with a bad case of hair, and too nervous to shave.

The balloon is ready. They get into the gondola. As soon as they are high enough they begin to beat the monkey again.

Finally thinking they have gone too far (the mountain hotel vacation, hiring a balloon), they retire to a small but well-located cabin on the coast of Maine.

After their landlord leaves, satisfied that they are comfortable, making his way down the rocky path, they once more continue beating the monkey.

They feel this place offers the proper privacy, with a particularly beautiful view of the coast . . .

After viewing the ocean for a while, smiling at their good choice of location, they turn once again to the monkey, which has been scheduled for another round of beatings . . .

Catastrophe at Sea

They had not been at sea for more than a few weeks when everything seemed to go wrong.

The Captain remarked in his log book that although they were meeting serious tests the crew were really quite a nice bunch, obedient to the letter, even though they were mostly illiterates.

After they lost the rudder and sails he had ordered the crew to their bunks; *best not to have them under foot.*

The Captain had been spending his time making toys for the crew to play with in their bunks; they are only allowed up to go to the head (sea-talk for bathroom).

Sometimes, writes the Captain in his log book, I tell them stories until they sleep.

Sooner or later we must meet an iceberg or a reef; meanwhile it is easier for one in the position of a father, as it were, in hopeless circumstances to reduce his grown sons, big hairy men most of them, into little children, lest they turn on me as men turn on God, for things that neither I nor God can be blamed for . . .

The last entry in the Captain's log book reads, I have run out of toys and stories; and what seemed to be scurvy turns out to be bedsores. There is a general restlessness and much crying in the crew's quarters. They fight over their toys. I have had to take harsh means, spanking them one by one over my knees.

Soon they will turn; my only hope is that we meet with an iceberg or a reef . . . We are running out of lollipops, and I am thinking of killing them one by one on the poop deck and dropping them into the ocean away from the sight of the others . . . I hate to start this because an iceberg or a reef might just turn up . . . Still, soon I must make a choice . . . Yet, I shouldn't want to sin unnecessarily . . .

Counting Sheep

A scientist has a test tube full of sheep. He wonders if he should try to shrink a pasture for them.

They are like grains of rice.

He wonders if it is possible to shrink something out of existence.

He wonders if the sheep are aware of their tininess, if they have any sense of scale. Perhaps they just think the test tube is a glass barn . . .

He wonders what he should do with them; they certainly have less meat and wool than ordinary sheep. Has he reduced their commercial value?

He wonders if they could be used as a substitute for rice, a sort of woolly rice . . .

He wonders if he just shouldn't rub them into a red paste between his fingers.

He wonders if they're breeding, or if any of them have died.

He puts them under a microscope and falls asleep counting them . . .

The Ambassador Visits Dr. Clutter

The Ambassador is put in a wheelbarrow, by way of trans-
portation.

What a quaint custom . . . , he begins to say as he's jerked
uphill to Dr. Clutter's laboratory.

Dr. Clutter, he is known to be a great devotee of marmalade,
constantly at the marmalade jar in neglect of his work. It is said
that he missed a Nobel prize by his too constant attention to the
marmalade jar.

As we approach Dr. Clutter's laboratory we sight Dr. Clutter
and see something on his upper lip.

On your upper lip, is that marmalade, Dr. Clutter?

No no, it's my mustache . . . I think . . . ?

Are you sure, Doctor?

He licks his upper lip. Hmmm, wait a minute . . .

Well, Doctor . . . ?

Well, I don't know; I'll have to analyze it. If you'll just wait
a minute I'll set up the equipment.

No no, it's no matter, Doctor.

No bother.

As he sets up the equipment to analyze what he has on his
upper lip he is all the time dipping marmalade with his fingers
from a jar, and we fail to see how he will be able to analyze what
he has on his upper lip because both his upper lip and chin, not
to mention his hands and all the lab equipment he's assembling,
are coated with sticky marmalade.

Doctor, with all that marmalade how can you find your
work?

Delicious stuff, he says, just love it!

But, the Ambassador . . . ?

That fellow in the wheelbarrow?

Yes.

Just let me have one more dip of marmalade . . . Perhaps two. I know it must look outrageously self-indulgent, and by all standards it really is; but you see, I really like marmalade . . . Could you possibly indulge me a third, and possibly a fourth dip? . . . And since we have come this far, a fifth and a sixth dip? . . . Perhaps I shall spend the rest of the day dipping marmalade . . . The fact is I don't think I shall find time to see the Ambassador today . . .

Is this how you lost the Nobel prize?

This is how I lost the prize . . . My wife . . . My self-respect . . . And some say, even my mind . . .

Poor Dr. Clutter . . .

We jerk the Ambassador down the hill to his embassy as he mumbles, what an odd fellow, what a very strange man is Dr. Clutter . . .

The International Neutering Commission

In the future, when men have joined biology with machinery, aeroplanes'll have babies; pink little ones with wet limp wings. Gasoline udders between her wheels, the maternal machine gives her baby suck . . .

Oh, but do be careful at rutting time, the males are dangerous; particularly martial aircraft. They'll bomb and strafe anything that moves; best not to wear red.

They are like insects that mate in the air, flying one on top of the other, like enormous darning needles. They're not afraid to die for it; often they crash.

And now commercial flights are dangerous courtships; airliners diving and looping in rituals of love; the people inside sick and frightened.

Airliners colliding in midair with monstrous thuds; a giant steel horn of a penis, covered with rivets, missing the female airliner's plastic vagina, comes through the floor of her fuselage: "Two airliners have collided in midair; all passengers are reported lost . . ."

Finally, an International Neutering Commission is set up to oversee the neutering of all aircraft.

This done, the sexual aeroplane soon becomes extinct, even as the aircraft industry begins to revive.

Some said that nature was not ready; to which others said, so what . . . ?

The Abyss

A dining room floats out into space . . .

On earth a cook with a large ham turns back. She calls across the abyss to the living room where people are waiting for dinner, sirs and ladies, I can't get the ham into the dining room . . .

Has the Cook suddenly developed a sense of humor?!
. . . I don't think she's so funny.

Sirs and ladies, I can't get the ham into the dining room . . . Shall I try the split pea soup? Maybe I could get some bread in . . . ? I'll try . . .

Just get the food on the table, and stop trying to be funny!
. . . I don't think she's so funny.
No no, I didn't mean she was successful, I meant she was trying to be funny.
Well, that's something, lots of cooks won't even try . . .

Sirs and ladies, I can't even get the bread into the dining room. Perhaps I could slip a few olives in . . . ? I'll try . . .

What in hell is she trying to pull?!—Olives?!—*She'll try to slip a few olives in?!* You'd better just cut the excuses, and get the dinner on the table!

Sirs and ladies, I can't find the dining room; I don't think it's in the house.

. . . Not in the house?! Have you ever heard of anything so silly?

She's certainly not clever, but she is trying, you've got to give her that.

But she wasn't hired to entertain us.

. . . Do you really think she is entertaining?

No no, I didn't mean she was entertaining, but for some odd reason she's trying to be. Perhaps she wants a raise . . . ?

Well, at least that's more than most cooks'll do, they all want raises; but how many of them really try to be entertaining?

Sirs and ladies, what shall I do . . . ?

Try singing; so far your performance is not very good!

. . . Can she sing?

Who knows? She's tried everything else, we might as well hear her sing . . .

The Feet of the Fat Man

The fat man is asked why he's so fat.

He claims to be only as fat as he needs to be; he doesn't think he's overdoing it . . .

How does one measure? Just being fat seems too much. On the other hand, accepting that there are fat people, how can one tell when a fat man is too fat?

Yet, this man is so fat that his head suddenly slips down into his neck. His face looks up out of his neck. He says, what do you think, do you think I'm overdoing it?

Now his shoulders and chest are slipping down into his stomach and hips—oh my God, he's beginning to fold down like porridge into his thighs!

He's definitely too fat, his bones won't support it.

God, he's going into his calves! His ankles are beginning to bulge.

When he finishes he's only a couple of feet all swollen out of shape.

In one of the feet where the ankle should start is his face. He says, what do you think, do you think I'm overdoing it?

We look into the other foot just to make sure he doesn't have another face; and we are pleasantly surprised to see hair, the foot is full of hair; which we take to be the other half of his head, the back half . . .

The Neighborhood Dog

A neighborhood dog is climbing up the side of a house.

I don't like to see that, I don't like to see a dog like that, says someone passing in the neighborhood.

The dog seems to be making for that 2nd story window. Maybe he wants to get his paws on the sill; he may want to hang there and rest; his tongue throbbing from his open mouth.
Yet, in the room attached to that window (the one just mentioned) a woman is looking at a cedar box; this is of course where she keeps her hatchet: in that same box, the one in this room, the one she is looking at.

That person passing in the neighborhood says, that dog is making for that 2nd story window . . . This is a nice neighborhood, that dog is wrong . . .

If the dog gets his paws on the sill of the window, which is attached to the same room where the woman is opening her hatchet box, she may chop at his paws with that same hatchet. She might want to chop at something; it is, after all, getting close to chopping time . . .

Something is dreadful, I feel a sense of dread, says that same person passing in the neighborhood, it's that dog that's not right, not that way . . .

In the room attached to the window that the dog has been making for, the woman is beginning to see two white paws on the sill of that same window, which is attached to the same room where that same woman is beginning to see two white paws on the sill of that same window, which looks out over the neighborhood.

She says, it's wrong . . . Something . . . The windowsill . . . Something . . . The windowsill . . .

She wants her hatchet. She thinks she's going to need it now . . .

The person passing in the neighborhood says, something may happen . . . That dog . . . I feel a sense of dread . . .

The woman goes to the hatchet in its box. She wants it. But it's gone bad. It's soft and nasty. It smells dead. She wants to get it out of its box (that same cedar box where she keeps it). But it bends and runs through her fingers . . .

Now the dog is coming down, crouched low to the wall, backwards; leaving a wet streak with its tongue down the side of the house.

And that same person passing in the neighborhood says, that dog is wrong . . . I don't like to see a dog get like that . . .

Turtles

Bales of turtles descend like floating oriental villages; and still they come, until the hills are only turtles, until there is no surface of the immediate earth that is not turtles. They cover the trunks of trees, the branches. They are everywhere!

People are forced to shovel their way in the roads; forced to shovel out their beds at night; only to awaken from dreaming endlessly of turtles, covered with turtles.

People become so distracted they no longer remember how to speak, they do not know words anymore; only *turtle*... They stare, their heads askew, whispering, turtle, turtle, turtle . . .

Nothing

. . . The Uncle repairs to the upstairs murmuring something about aspirins and bunion pads . . .

Strange old unmarried Uncle with his pipe and mustache, his glasses, his reading of newspapers; sips coffee all day and sucks his teeth; used to collect butterflies and stamps; used to wake up at night screaming, I didn't do it! I didn't do it! . . . has been sleeping quietly for the last few years . . .

Now he is returning. He is heard on the stairs. He is entering the room; no doubt to resume his newspaper, or to suck his teeth; perhaps he will prepare his pipe and light it; perhaps he'll fish out his pocket watch and wind it, listening for its tick . . .

But this time Uncle comes into the room dressed in his little niece's white dress, his hairy legs showing through her long white stockings. He even has her hair ribbon tied in his own thinning hair . . .

Well, folks, how do I look? he says to his sister and her husband.

His brotherinlaw says, no good.

His sister says, no no, dear, it does nothing for you.

Nothing for me?

Nothing.

Time of the King

There was a king who didn't like to wait very much. When a pleasant date was approaching he would simply do away with the days or weeks that stood between.

ALL CITIZENS ARE ASKED TO X ALL THE DAYS ON THEIR CALENDARS BETWEEN NOW AND THE KING'S PLEASURE.

At other times the king might insist on re-playing a particular date representing some high satisfaction: IT WILL BE MAY 13, 1974 FOR TWO WEEKS, OR UNTIL FURTHER NOTICE.

Sometimes the king, in moods of having nothing to look forward to, would reverse the calendar to dates of former pleasures. Sometimes he would remain in the past for years.

One day he settled into childhood, just on the edge of puberty, just when he was discovering the joys of masturbation.

No no, that looks bad, said one of his high advisers.

What's so bad about a kid having a little fun? Freud says it's normal, said the distracted king.

After a year of masturbating the king became very depressed and decided he didn't want to live anymore.

The king consulted insurance company actuarials, had medical advice as to his general health, checked the longevity of his ancestors, and put all of this through a computer, arriving at a date when he might reasonably expect to die of *natural* causes; had new calendars printed describing a year many years away; and specifying a month and a day in that future year, went to bed and died.

The Fisherman,
or When Things Go Amiss

I like to go down where the fishermen prepare their nets; early morning and the fog is beginning to burn clear. A bearded fisherman, with hands worked coarse by rope and salt, repairs his net and smokes his pipe. He says, I can't remember when it was I didn't have to do with fishing boats; my father was a fisher, and his father too.

It must be wonderful to know what to do, I said.

Well, it's I was born to it, he said.

And this is all you've ever done? I said.

Well, I used to be a wee little Miss, as my parents took me wrong; until at thirty my parents said, hey looky, the little girl's got her a fine bunch of whisker hairs, he said.

You mean they took you to be a woman?

Why, they most surely did, and it was toe dancing I learned . . . That fisherman over there, the one with the pipe and whiskers, he was my husband . . .

I can hardly believe that you were once a woman.

It's I was got off to a wrong start, and before I knew it I was married and was got myself a little pregnant, too, he said.

A little pregnant?!

And you shoulda seen what a sight I was; me with this beard, and belly all swollup, smoking my pipe and waddling around . . .

Smoking your pipe . . . ?

Why, sure. I been smoking this pipe since my first whiskers. A man what can grow whiskers, says my father, has title to pipe and whiskey.

But how could you get married to another man? I asked.

I was got all fitted up in one of them fancy wedding gowns; and then the preacher put the words and I was got myself married. I remember the preacher saying, get rid of that pipe. My mother grabbed it out of my mouth . . .

What about the baby? I asked.

This is him, he said as he pulled an infant out of his pea jacket. Then he unbuttoned his shirt and gave it suck.

Then you are a woman, I said.

Well, yes and no; I'm a man who was got off to a wrong start, and was a wee little Miss what did toe dancing . . .

I don't go down to where the fishermen prepare their nets anymore; there's something distressingly inexact about who or what they are . . . Who they seem to be in no way tells who they are, or might have been; or, in fact, what they may yet become in future.

When the God Returns

When the God returns he gives the world to mannequins and toys. Dummies in store windows receive the world as though the world had always been theirs. Dolls that children played with are suddenly the masters; families are consigned to shelves and playrooms.

The world crawls with motherless toys that murmur, mama. Naked female mannequins, without vaginas, walk the roads at night like human ghosts . . .

A Raggedy Ann confronts a family at dinner. The painted smile is suddenly full of small animal teeth. She orders them out of the dining room into a closet.

They must obey.

She wants to cut mother's head off. She wants to cut father's penis off. She wants to open junior to see what's inside of junior.

They must obey . . .

Breakfast at Sea

Some wealthy people seeking a seaward recreation have hired a yacht. Captain Happiness and a small crew are charged with all matters pertaining to the flotation and propulsion of this same yacht. Deep in some dark recess of the yacht's hull Cooky, the cook, mans the galley . . .

Now we find them at sea, first morning out, early, the earth addressing the sun, low in the east; breakfast time.

Cooky somewhere deep in the hull; perhaps frantic to keep ahead of the expected avalanche of appetites, begins to cook all manner of breakfast foods: Cereals in all their variety, sugar- and smoke-cured meats, eggs in all the ways they are cooked; not to forget pancakes and waffles, and all the list of breadstuffs . . . Jams and honey, syrups and butter; fruit and fruit juices . . .

But, somehow, breakfast is getting all over the ship. The Captain has marmalade on his white uniform. There's marmalade smeared all over the ship's wheel!

How did those fried eggs get all over the deck?

Why are sausages confused in the anchor chain?

Why is all that porridge coming up from below deck?

Who put those maple syrup covered waffles all over the deck chairs?

Is there any reason for all that bacon to be hanging along the deck rails?

The rudder is jammed with ham!

The engine room's flooded with hot chocolate!

Captain Happiness comes to the wealthy people, who are in the first morning of their seaward recreation, and says, I give up, I don't understand it; all those fried eggs . . .

Well, don't give up the ship, Captain . . .

I just don't get it, says the Captain.

But, Captain, what are we to do?

I haven't the foggiest . . .

But, Captain, you're supposed to be a professional man of the sea, we're only landlubbers, so to speak . . . But this breakfast at sea, if you don't mind our saying, seems to have gotten quite out of hand . . .

That's what I mean, I don't understand it either; I'm just a ship's captain, I don't understand this breakfast thing; it's not natural . . .

But, Captain . . .

Stop nagging me! Surely you can see how upset I am?

But, Captain . . .

Stop annoying me about details! Surely you can see that I have a ship to run?! I can't spend the whole day going over the breakfast menu, I have too many things to do. I have to get this marmalade off my uniform. The hot chocolate has to be pumped out of the engine room. And then there's lunch to contend with; not to mention supper, which, unfortunately, is the largest meal of the day . . .

The Pipe Smokers

Some men are smoking pipes. The room has grown thick with their blue exhalations. Their wives and other villagers stand outside looking in through the windows.

Some of the pipe smokers lean on canes, others rest their elbows on the mantelpiece. One sits on the arm of a couch; still another, with his arms folded, leans against a wall puffing his pipe.

Every so often a match is ignited into a bright orange flame through the blue smoke, and a pipe is relighted, the flame pulsing at the bowl.

Now one of the pipe smokers is lighting his pipe again. The people at the windows are watching him. He has a wooden match. He is about to strike it. He does strike it. A bright orange flame hovers at the bowl of his pipe.

His pipe has caught fire. He's in trouble. The people at the window are watching.

The bowl of his pipe is now entirely consumed, and the fire is working up the stem toward his face.

In a few minutes his face is on fire. First, his overhanging nose and brows, and then his cheeks; his fedora, first the brim, then flames are all over the crown. His whole head is burning.

One of his hands fumbles in a pocket searching for a fresh pipe. But the flames are all over his shoulders and running down his arms.

He finally pulls a fresh pipe out, but the flames quickly find it.

Now his trousers and shoes are on fire.

Luckily he is one of the pipe smokers who were leaning on the mantelpiece. His burnt-out body crumbles to the hearth-stone with an empty granular thud.

Suddenly the pipe smoking period is over. All pipes are knocked, bowls down, along the mantelpiece. Pipe ashes with the burnt-out body of their fellow pipe smoker are kicked into the fireplace.

The pipe smokers leave. The people at the windows turn away . . .

A Brother's Description/A Night Song

A man spends all his money on a pair of shoes; takes them home and looks at them; decides against keeping them; sets out at midnight for the shoe store; waits in the darkness for the shoe store to open; at 9 A.M. enters and begs the salesman to take the shoes back; goes down on his knees, and is returned his money.

This same man now buys an expensive hat with the money; takes it home; becomes dissatisfied with it and returns it in like manner as the shoes: goes down on his knees and begs his money back.

Refunded his money, he once more returns to the shoe store and explains that he has made a grave mistake and now wishes to buy back the shoes; goes down on his knees; is sold the shoes again.

Taking them home he once more discovers that he is in possession of shoes he doesn't want; once more sets out with a view to getting his money back and buying back the same hat he returned the day before. But halfway there in the darkness decides against it; starts for home; nearly home decides again to return the shoes; starts toward town; partway there decides against returning the shoes; starts again toward home; decides against it; turns, starts toward town; turns, starts toward home; turns, starts toward town; falls in the road in the early morning dew, crying . . .

A Roof with Some Clouds Behind It

A man is climbing what he thinks is the ladder of success. He's got the idea, says father.

Yes, he seems to know the direction, says mother.

But you do realize that some men have gone quite the other way and brought up gold? says father.

Then you think he would do better in the earth? says mother.

I have a terrible feeling that he's on the wrong ladder, says father.

But he's still in the right direction, isn't he? says mother.

Yes, but, you see, there seems to be only a roof with some clouds behind it at the top of the ladder, says father.

Hmmm, I never noticed that before, how strange. I wonder if that roof and those clouds realize that they're in the wrong place? says mother.

I don't think they're doing it on purpose, do you? says father.

No, probably just a thoughtless mistake, says mother.

Then their son reaches the top of the ladder and is shouting down to his parents, mommy, daddy, success!

Do you think we should tell him? says mother.

No, let him enjoy it while he can, says father.

Then mother shouts up to her son, enjoy it while you can, honey.

While I can? he shouts down.

While you still don't notice that it's only a roof with some clouds behind it, she shouts.

Okay, he shouts down, while I still don't notice that it's only a roof with some clouds behind it I'll enjoy it while I can.

And remember, son, you can always go into the earth! screams his father.

The Howling

A large woman has killed her parakeet with an ax; went suddenly berserk; blood all over the house, splashed all over the neighborhood, on the roads leading out of town. It is said that parakeet blood was found in several neighboring towns; that it was even splashed several states away!

She was known to love birds; would put food out in the winter for them.

Her neighbors are curious about her, this large woman who lived alone with a parakeet.

She is splattered with blood. She doesn't seem to see all the people who have gathered to watch her being taken out of her house.

The ax comes out in a bloody burlap bag. The body of the parakeet follows on a rubber stretcher.

The large woman does not seem to see the people who have gathered to watch the authorities lead her out of her house; even as the ax comes out in a blood-soaked burlap bag; the body of the parakeet on a rubber stretcher.

Thin sheets of blood run from the upstairs windows down the walls of the house.

Every so often a tide of blood pours down the stairs from the 2nd floor, and gushes through the front door over the porch, down the front walk into the street.

Someone says the cellar is waist-deep in blood.

The large woman, her arms being held, is led out of her house, down the steps of her front porch into the front yard of her house; people have gathered to watch, even as the ax is carried out in a bloody sack of burlap; two men carrying the parakeet out on a rubber stretcher . . .

Suddenly the large woman begins to howl with a sound deep in herself; it grows loud and awful.

The people stand away. The authorities let go of her arms and begin to back away.

Blood oozes up out of the grass, and drops of blood roll down the telephone poles in long red strokes . . .

The Fear of Falling

There was a cow named Emile who had climbed up a drain pipe to the roof of a house to eat a bird which was on the roof.

Now Emile seeing that the roof slants dangerously on both sides of its ridge regrets her appetite, longing for the relative flat of the pasture, where simple nourishment grows at one's feet.

Emile is now nibbling the shingles of the roof hoping to bite a hole into the attic. And yes, Emile's industry is making just such a hole. And Emile is falling down into the attic and through the attic floor; she is crashing through the ceiling of Farmer Blink's bedroom, and falling on Farmer Blink in his bed.

Farmer Blink blinks with surprise. Farmer Blink says, I didn't know you cared.

Emile doesn't care, not even a little; but Emile must pretend to care because it hides Emile's foolishness.

Then you do care a little? says Farmer Blink.

No, Emile does not care for Farmer Blink, not even a little. But Emile starts to lick Farmer Blink's face because Emile cannot tell Farmer Blink that Emile went on the roof to eat a bird who, when Emile got on the roof, flew away.

But then Mrs. Farmer Blink comes in and starts to beat at Emile, and Emile is scrambling to the door, slipping and sliding and lowing, it is all a terrible misunderstanding!

And now Mrs. Farmer Blink is beating Farmer Blink, and he has many tears around his eyes; and he is screaming, please do not hurt me anymore.

Emile is so sorry to have done this terrible thing; and she is lowing, it was the bird, yes, the bird, and the fear of falling, which is so basic . . .

Mr. & Mrs. Duck Dinner

An old woman with a duck under her arm is let into a house and asked, whom shall I say is calling?

Mr. and Mrs. Duck Dinner.

If you don't mind my asking, which is which?

Pointing to the duck the old woman says, this here's my husband.

A little time passes and the butler reappears, yes, come right in, you're expected, the kitchen's just this way.

In the kitchen there's a huge stove. The butler says, I'm sorry, we don't have a pot big enough for you; so we're using an old cast-iron bathtub. I hope you don't mind? We have a regular duck pot for your husband.

No no, this is fine, I'll make pretend I'm having a bath.—Oh, by the way, do you have enough duck sauce? says the old woman.

Yes, plenty, and the cook's made up a nice stuffing, too.

My husband'll need plucking; I can undress myself, says the old woman.

Fine, that'll be a great help; we'll have the kitchen girl defeather your husband.—By the way, what would you suggest with duck? asks the butler.

Wild rice, but not too wild, we wouldn't want any trouble in the dining room; and perhaps asparagus spears . . . But make sure they're not too sharp, they can be quite dangerous; best to dull them on a grinding wheel before serving . . .

Very good, Madam.—By the way, do you think that having the kitchen girl defeather your husband might be a little awkward, if you know what I mean? She is rather pretty; wouldn't want to start any difficulties between you and your husband, says the butler.

No worry, says the old woman, we're professional duck

dinners; if we started fooling around with the kitchen help we'd soon be out of business.—If you don't mind I'd like to get into the oven as soon as possible. I'm not as young as I used to be, not that I'm that old, but it does take me a little longer these days . . .

The Explosion at the Club

The ape is accepted, and sits quietly smoking a cigar and reading a newspaper, which he holds upside down.

This is all after the commotion . . .

And so the ape begins a career at the club of sipping scotch and flicking ashes from his cigars.

Someone says, he does seem a decent chap . . .

And yes, the ape is blending quite nicely with the paneled walls and leather chairs. One has to look quite carefully to pick out the 600 pounds of animal flesh.

And many club evenings pass, the ape lost in a moth landscape of newspapers poised at the financial news . . .

Someone says of the ape, he's really not a bad fellow, he minds his own business . . .

Then one evening the ape's head explodes like a small cannon going off.

All the gentlemen turn to see what the great beast has been up to.

Out of the place where its head should start are uncoiled clock springs exploded out of its neck like a battered rooster's tail.

Someone says, I never did like him, always had a feeling there was something funny about him . . .

The Ascension of the Cow

The cow that goes to heaven must take its body for not having enough brain to remember itself in spirit.

It is an unhappy time of struggle. The cow mooing. It is no less difficult than a breech birth.

But if the cow should die it must be raised toward heaven, lest it perish in forgetfulness, the sleep of pastures.

The farmer is trying to get the cow into the hayloft, *nearer, my God, to Thee,* pulling the cow with ropes; the cow trying to get a footing over the tractor and bales of hay piled for the ascension . . .

—The cow mooing, the farmer praying, and his wife crying, scandal, scandal, scandal!

The Hemorrhoid Epidemic

They kill the man's monkey because they think it has infected the neighborhood with hemorrhoids.

The man thinks the monkey too good to waste, even if there is only enough monkey to make one boot.

And so he has one boot made, and calls this his monkey-boot.

The boot reminds him of his monkey; the fur on it is exactly like the fur on his monkey.

But, why not, he thinks, is it not made from the same monkey whose fur is like the fur on his boot?

But since there is only one boot he decides he'll either have to have one of his legs amputated or have the boot made into a hat.

He decides to have the boot made into a hat because he has only one head and will not have to have one of his heads amputated.

But when the boot has been made into a hat he doesn't know whether to call it his boot-hat or his monkey-hat.

The hat reminds him of a boot he once had.

But why shouldn't it, he thinks, was it not once a boot?

But that boot reminds him of a monkey he once had.

Yet, why should it not, he thinks, was it not made from the same monkey that it reminds him of?

He is puzzled.

Meanwhile, the hemorrhoid epidemic continues to spread . . .

Far from the Bureaucracy of Heaven

He was ladling water from one bucket to another. But he noticed that the level of water in one bucket was getting lower, even as the level in the other was rising.

He wondered whose fault this was.

He decided to allow the water to rise in the bucket that the water was rising in anyway, and see about the other bucket's level after the first bucket was fully served.

When the bucket was full he said, now stay full while I see to your brother.

He began to ladle water from the full bucket into the empty one. He saw the water rising in the formerly empty bucket. He took this as an excellent sign that the bucket was recovering.

Yet, he could not help noticing that the level was falling in the other bucket. He said, can't you wait a minute while I tend to your brother?

But the level continued to fall even as its brother bucket seemed well on its way to a full recovery.

When the bucket was full he began to ladle the water the other way. And again he noticed that the full bucket was losing its water even as the empty bucket was beginning to recover.

He scratched his head and wondered whose fault this was; wondering if this was not after all another of those meaningless cruelties happening far from the Bureaucracy of Heaven?

A New Life

The Gentlemen in the Meadow

Some gentlemen are floating in the meadow over the yellow grass. They seem to hover by those wonderful blue little flowers that grow there by those rocks.

Perhaps they have floated up from that nearby graveyard? They drift a little when the wind blows.

Butterflies flutter through them . . .

Goodnight

A man parks his car; and as he gets out the car says, goodnight.

Did you speak to me? says the man, not sure that he has not spoken to himself.

I said goodnight, says the car.

Well then, says the man, goodnight to you, too.

Sleep well, says the car.

Sleep well? chuckles the man. Thank you . . .

May all your dreams come true, says the car.

My dreams are not always good ones . . .

I mean the good ones, says the car.

You're very thoughtful; why have you never spoken before? says the man.

Oh, I don't know, says the car, perhaps it's just that I feel a little lonely tonight.

. . . I know, sometimes that feeling comes over me, says the man.

Well, have a good rest, and perhaps I'll see you tomorrow, says the car.

And you, too . . . Goodnight, says the man as he walks away.

The Marionettes of Distant Masters

A pianist dreams that he's hired by a wrecking company to ruin a piano with his fingers . . .

On the day of the piano wrecking concert, as he's dressing, he notices a butterfly annoying a flower in his window box. He wonders if the police should be called. Then he thinks maybe the butterfly is just a marionette being manipulated by its master from the window above.

Suddenly everything is beautiful. He begins to cry.

Then another butterfly begins to annoy the first butterfly. He again wonders if he shouldn't call the police.

But, perhaps they are marionette-butterflies? He thinks they are, belonging to rival masters seeing whose butterfly can annoy the other's the most.

And this is happening in his window box. The Cosmic Plan: Distant Masters manipulating minor Masters who, in turn, are manipulating tiny Butterfly-Masters who, in turn, are manipulating him . . . A universe webbed with strings!

Suddenly it is all so beautiful; the light is strange . . . Something about the light! He begins to cry . . .

One Morning

One morning a man awakens to find strings coming through his window attached to his hands and feet.

. . . I'm not a marionette, he says, his voice rising with the question, am I? Am I a marionette?

One of the strings loosens and jerks as he scratches his head.

. . . Hmmm, he says, I just wonder if I am a marionette?

And then all the strings pull and jerk and he is jumping out of bed.

Now that he's up he'll just go to the window and see who's doing tricks with him when he's half asleep . . .

He follows the strings up into the sky with his eyes and sees a giant hand sticking through a cloud, holding a crossbar to which the strings are attached . . .

Hmmm, he says, that's funny, I never saw that crossbar before . . . I guess I am a marionette . . .

Old Women

There was an old woman who kept another old woman as a pet in her backyard, chained to a tree near a bowl of water.

Then another old woman visited the first old woman and spoke of another old woman who had spoken of still another old woman.

Oh, how interesting, said the first old woman to the visiting old woman.

Then the visiting old woman looked out of the window and said, oh, what a lovely old pet chained to a tree.

Oh, that is my pet old woman, said the first old woman.

Oh, what a lovely old pet, said the visiting old woman.

The Judgment

A man dresses up like a judge and stands before a mirror and sentences himself to loneliness for the rest of his life.

But, your Honor, you haven't heard my side of it . . .

You have no *side* of it; you have been found guilty of impersonating a judge and standing before a mirror admiring yourself.

I throw myself on the mercy of the court; I acted only out of loneliness . . .

Loneliness is no excuse for violating the law.

But, your Honor, please, I've been lonely all my life. Isn't the debt almost paid?—Not more loneliness!—I demand my sentence be shortened! I've already paid for my crime!

I make no deals with convicted criminals. If you think you can do better try another judge.

But, your Honor . . .

Clear the court and go to bed!

The Dog

A dog hangs in a kitchen, his back stuck to the ceiling. An old woman tries to work him loose with the handle of her broom.

The dog struggles, but the more he struggles the deeper he sinks into the ceiling. He growls and snaps. He implores and whines, swallowing and chewing; his tongue curling in and out of his mouth, as though he lapped water . . .

Finally only the dark little dots of his footpads can be seen. They hear him whining inside the ceiling . . .

The dog . . . ? says the old woman.
The dog is ruined, says her husband.
The dog . . . ? says the old woman.
It's the ceiling, says her husband.
The dog . . . ? says the old woman.
It ate the dog, the ceiling ate the dog, says her husband.
The dog . . . ? says the old woman.
. . . The dog, says the old man.

The Old Woman's Breakfast

The old woman at breakfast, she is so weary she hardly tells herself from the porridge she eats.

She can't tell if she spoons the porridge into herself, or herself into the porridge . . .

The walls melt, and her mind seems to float all over the room like a puff of dust slapped out of a pillow.

She falls into the porridge, she becomes part of it.

She is a porridge of melting walls; her bones no longer different than her flesh, her eyes no longer different than her nostrils . . . She begins to spill over the edge of the table . . .

The Pilot

Up in a dirty window in a dark room is a star which an old man can see. He looks at it. He can see it. It is the star of the room; an electrical freckle that has fallen out of his head and gotten stuck in the dirt on the window.

He thinks he can steer by that star. He thinks he can use the back of a chair as a ship's wheel to pilot this room through the night.

He says to himself, brave Captain, are you afraid?

Yes, I am afraid; I am not so brave.

Be brave, my Captain.

And all night the old man steers his room through the dark . . .

Grass

The living room is overgrown with grass. It has come up around the furniture. It stretches through the dining room, past the swinging door into the kitchen. It extends for miles and miles into the walls . . .

There's treasure in grass, things dropped or put there; a stick of rust that was once a penknife, a grave marker . . . All hidden in the grass at the scalp of the meadow . . .

In a cellar under the grass an old man sits in a rocking chair, rocking to and fro. In his arms he holds an infant, the infant body of himself. And he rocks to and fro under the grass in the dark . . .

Hands

An old woman buys an ape's hand for supper. It will not be still, it keeps clenching and unclenching its fist. It might want to pinch her too, she thinks.

Be still, you silly thing, while I clean your fingernails. She wants to clean it up and pluck the fur off it to make it ready for the pot.

She doesn't know whether she'll fry it or boil it, or just simply hurt it, stick it with a fork or a hat pin. She'll hurt it if it doesn't be still!

Be still, you silly thing!

Now the ape's hand is pointing with its forefinger to the cupboard.

The cupboard, huh?

And she is trying to see the angle of the forefinger to see where it points. It points high, something at the top of the cupboard.

What's there? She starts to climb the cupboard, using the shelves as a ladder.

What's up here so grand to be pointed at?

The ape's hand has become a fist and is pounding the table.

I'm looking for it! Stop pounding the table, you silly thing!

The ape's fist continues to pound; the room shakes with it.

Please, please, I'll fall, cries the old woman.

At the top of the cupboard she finds an old dried-out hand covered with dust.

Is this what you want?

The ape's hand on the table opens and closes, as if it would grasp what she has found; and then pounds the table as if to say, hurry, hurry, bring it down to me!

All right, all right, I'm coming.

Finally she puts the dried-out hand into the ape's hand. The ape's hand lays the dried-out hand on its back, and strokes the insides of the fingers and palm, until the hand begins to be alive. Then the two hands close into a clasped set, the short blunt thumbs twirling at each other . . .

The old woman sits watching the hands, with their short blunt thumbs twirling, late into the night, until she falls asleep in her chair . . .

The Hand Squeezing

An old woman marries a young infant.

She is dressed in white; he in a formal black diaper.

They stand before the minister; she leans on a cane, the bridegroom lies on a pillow being held by his nurse, screaming.

Rice is thrown, and the couple is driven away on their honeymoon.

Oh, how perfectly beautiful, weeps the mother of the groom.

Her husband squeezes her hand.

Don't do that, that hurts! she screams.

He says, I didn't mean to hurt you, I only meant to make a gesture of solidarity, that, whereas we have lost our son to the most normal longing that a young man can have, still, we have each other . . .

That doesn't give you any reason to hurt me! she screamed.

But dear, I didn't mean to hurt you; honestly, honey . . .

The Little Lady

A female hand puppet refuses to let the puppet master put his hand up under her dress.

No no, it is too embarrassing, she weeps.

Oh please, little lady, my hand is your life, says the puppet master.

Oh no, that cannot be, she weeps, have I no other life except indignity?

I assure you, little lady, there's nothing *there.*

Nothing there . . . ? she weeps. Surely I'm not without woman's treasure?

Only a tunnel of pretty cloth; the passage where I put my hand to make you dance.

. . . But you haven't said you love me.

Please, little lady . . .

No no, we'll have to be married first, that's only fair, she weeps.

And so the puppet master makes up another of the puppets into a little justice of the peace, and has him perform the marriage.

Now, little lady . . . ?

Now, and *forever,* my love, she says with the puppet master making her voice with his falsetto . . .

An Old Eclair and Its Artichoke

An old eclair and its artichoke, as the old couple are wont to call each other, lie naked in the dark caressing the genitals of the other; kissing and whispering.

They float at night like clouds. Everything perishes, they think, except the love they have for each other, this old eclair and its artichoke, as they are wont to call each other, caressing the genitals of the other, kissing and whispering in the dark . . .

Baloney

A large person begins to wonder if I'm going to help him to The Baloney House, that restaurant just there, across the street.

He says, I have just been wondering if you're going to help me across the street to that restaurant? Do you see it? It's that one there, The Baloney House. I would like to have a baloney sandwich. I might want to have two baloney sandwiches. I'm very fond of baloney. You don't mind, do you, that I'm very fond of baloney? I admit I am rather partial to it.

Then I am wondering why he wants me to help him to The Baloney House. He seem very capable of managing it on his own . . .

I have just been wondering, he says again, if you're going to help me to The Baloney House? That restaurant just there, across the street. I'm rather partial, as you may have guessed, to baloney. I hope you don't mind?

No, not at all—but why do you need me to get you to The Baloney House?

It's a matter of a proper entrance. I shouldn't want the other baloney eaters at The Baloney House thinking I go about without someone who cares for me. Nor could I allow them to see me eating my baloney sandwiches thinking, what a lonely glutton, wallowing in baloney and his own juicy spit. I must have them think that you, at least, enjoy watching my mastications, because, of all things strange, you have come to love me . . . You see, sir, one is safe only when others think he is loved . . .

Dr. Nigel Bruce Watson Counting

Dr. Nigel Bruce Watson sat before a long piece of sunlight on the floor described by a French door as a series of golden oblongs, three wide and six down.

As he worked his ear for wax he discovered that his ear was loose. He absentmindedly tried to press it back, but it was hanging from his head.

It finally dropped on his shoulder. He tried pasting it back with marmalade which he had been eating for breakfast.

Now he had marmalade all over the side of his head; but the ear refused to stay in place. He put the ear in a cigarette box.

He touched his other ear, and it was also loose.

Better not fool with it, he thought.

But he absentmindedly touched it again, and it fell on his shoulder.

He tried pasting it back with marmalade. But this ear, like the first, refused to adhere.

He put the second ear with the first in the cigarette box, and murmured, I can hear perfectly well without those moth wings.

But now he had great patches of marmalade on the sides of his head. He decided to rub marmalade all over his head and face.

We'll just see what Holmes makes of this, he murmured.

And so Dr. Nigel Bruce Watson, eating marmalade for breakfast, and sitting, as stated, before a long piece of sunlight on the floor, thought best, then, to count the oblongs that made up the larger oblong, which the French door had been describing during the marmalade incident . . .

Now Dr. Nigel Bruce Watson, his head covered with marmalade, his ears in a cigarette box, begins to count . . .

The Gingerbread Woman

An old woman wishes she could climb into her own basket, like a gingerbread woman, the one who would have naturally married the gingerbread man, had they been made with more detail in their genital areas.

. . . How nice to lie in a basket on a linen napkin, near a pot of jam and a chicken leg, being kissed by a gingerbread man . . . Summer shadow, summer light, branch sway . . . Delight!

The Dog's Dinner

An old woman was just cooking her dog's dinner when she decided to review the general decline of things in her west window.

Yes, there the old sun bleeds and dies of childbirth.

In the east the anemic child rises, stillborn . . .

When she turns back to the pot where she cooks her dog's dinner she discovers that it is her dog that she is cooking for her dog's dinner.

How strange that when cooking a dog's dinner one cooks the very dog for whom the dinner was being cooked . . .

She takes the steaming pot off the stove and puts it on the floor, thinking that the dog will not be having its dinner tonight, thinking that the dog cannot eat itself . . .

She draws a chair to the pot, and sits there soaking her feet, seeing her dog floating at her ankles in the mist that rises from his dinner.

She thinks, if I cooked the dog, how is it I didn't cook myself? . . . Perhaps next time . . . ?

A New Life

An old man is dressed up like a gorilla and put in a forest full of gorillas, who take him as one of their own.

Soon he is deep into the gorilla life; married, as the gorillas do it, to a young female, who already swells with his child.

He must blame his gorilla costume for his high suçcess as a *gorilla* among gorillas.

What foresight of the costume-maker to have sewn a bladder of gorilla sperm in his gorilla pants.

What a thrilling sight, gorillas all under the moon in a circle holding hands, singing gorilla songs and dancing the gorilla dance: Lump-tiddi-do, lump-tiddi-do, lump-tiddi-do . . .

The Intuitive Journey

The Bell in the Forest

. . . I hear a bell ringing in a forest, a doorbell ringing in the earth under the trees.

I see between the trees, like moving mist, the frosted window of a front door; an umbrella stand standing among the trees, covered with moss. A man with a mustache, wearing a derby, is being let in. He shakes his umbrella outside the door. A woman takes it with his coat and derby. He rubs his hands and remarks something about the weather . . .

And then everything collapses under tons of earth and roots!

A distant doorbell rings in the earth. A man wearing a derby, holding an umbrella, appears, as if through the mist, at the frosted window of a door . . . The clop-clop and rounding hard sound of wheels on stone, a horse and buggy going past the house . . .

Suddenly the sky crumbles under the weight of the earth; the street with the horse and buggy, the vestibule of the house, are covered with roots and darkness!

In a forest under the roots of trees a doorbell is ringing, and a man wearing a derby appears between the trees through the mist in grey silhouette, as seen through the frosted window of a door . . .

A bell ringing in a forest under the trees . . .

The Canoeing

We went upstairs in a canoe. I kept catching my paddle in the banisters.

We met several salmon passing us, flipping step by step; no doubt to find the remembered bedroom. And they were like the slippered feet of someone falling down the stairs, played backward as in a movie.

And then we were passing over the downstairs closet under the stairs, and could feel the weight of dark overcoats and galoshes in a cave of umbrellas and fedoras; water dripping there, deep in the earth, like an endless meditation . . .

. . . Finally the quiet waters of the upstairs hall. We dip our paddles with gentle care not to injure the quiet dark, and seem to glide for days by family bedrooms under a stillness of trees . . .

The Overlap of Worlds

The furniture is like models of animals. You can see the dining room table as a kind of bull standing with its cows, the chairs. Or the easy chair with its footstool, the cow with its calf . . .

And they live a life, as if a spirit world and this were overlapped, oblivious to the other.

In moonlight these animals soften and resume their lives, browsing the rugs; as we, upstairs, asleep in our dreams, resume our lives; overlapping and oblivious to the other . . .

One Who Journeys in a Tree

FOR DAVID IGNATOW

In the tree the stairway of osmosis—up up through trunk to branch, thinner branch, out out into a twig, a leaf—expire!

I should love to photosynthesize in one leaf lost at the top of a tree. To be useful for no reason at all . . .

A door in a tree. A stairway that grows thinner and thinner into the narrowing of a twig; one diminishes, as it were, into a journey. The traveler dying down into a journey that ingests him until he is only the journey and those distances that you cannot see . . .

The trunk of this tree looks thick enough to hold a spiral stairway. I open the bark door and step in, and am suddenly at peace. As I climb the stairs with a kind of spiritual sweetness I know that I ruin myself; I grow smaller as the stairs narrow, like the traveler who diminishes in the diminishing road; and I do not call this dying, but metamorphosis . . .

In the Forest

I was combing some long hair coming out of a tree . . .

I had noticed long hair coming out of a tree, and a comb on the ground by the roots of that same tree.

The hair and the comb seemed to belong together. Not so much that the hair needed combing, but the reassurance of the comb being drawn through it . . .

I stood in the gloom and silence that many forests have in the pages of fiction, combing the thick womanly hair, the mammal-warm hair; even as the evening slowly took the forest into night . . .

The Lighted Window

A lighted window floats through the night like a piece of paper in the wind.

I want to see into it. I want to climb through into its lighted room.

As I reach for it it slips through the trees. As I chase it it rolls and tumbles into the air and skitters on through the night . . .

The Captain's Surprise

A Film-Script

The ship is ready. I step aboard. *(Keep the camera on me.)*

The Captain, a poor actor, is applauding a sea gull for the remarkable feat of flying over his ship. Did you see that? he cries. Nature has finally invented a creature that can fly!

I have myself seen gulls fly many times; and I wonder at the legitimacy of the Captain's surprise. *(I hope you have the right lens, this is a close-up.)*

I wonder if the Captain has the proper license for surprise? And even if he has, whether it's up to date and properly stamped by the Commissioner of Surprises?

Perhaps the Captain merely tries to draw the camera away from me?

Even so, one must wonder how he handles the great iceberg that looms in front of our ship one night.

Does he hold his cocktail in front of his drunken eyes and see only another piece of ice floating in his glass?

Something is happening below deck. *(Have the camera pan down into the galley to pick up the cook having intercourse with a large pile of fresh dough.)*

(In closing, pull the camera up into the clouds. Show the whole ship. To give the picture a sense of motion make sure the wake is full of white foam; if necessary, this can be painted in later.)

Layer by Layer

The artists come, and a picture of my ape is drawn . . .

. . . Things are different now, the noise of my ape is full of mourning doves. Something is missing, as if, somehow, a layer had been lifted away . . .

I want to say something. I need to say something!

I aim an unloaded camera at the ape and flick the shutter, and flick the shutter, and flick the shutter, watching the ape drifting slowly down through its layers, like something falling thousands of miles into itself . . .

Someone speaks in the distance. It is myself, the center drifting. The voice says, look, look, see what I have done to my ape . . . please!

But it's too late; when I return I realize suddenly that I am not anyone anymore; and I begin to fall down into my flesh, layer by layer, past the bone, into the secret marshlands of the marrow . . .

. . . Thousands of people were standing on the hills overlooking an abyss . . .

In Here

It's dark in here. I light it by thinking of light.

No one can tell me anything about this place, because I haven't got ears; until I think of ears. But it's always too late, I get too far away; which may only be an inch from the last whisper.

The light dims and dies, and I must think again, imagining the skull as a lantern. The eyes lit with candle. The teeth like church windows, alive with light.

The light goes down; and yet there is something in that, too. I begin to think of darkness in terms of texture; another kind of light, the light that shines inside the darkness . . .

Invent, invent, until the brain goes soft and sweet, like the old grandmother smiling in her sleep . . .

Song of the Cow

A cow browsing a field thinks, I eat grass . . . Hooves, they are not uncomfortable. The horns, I suppose, are the particular feature that marks us in the beasthood. We browsers, whose teeth are blunted for grass, grow out horns from our heads; the giant teeth of our brains, where we fear the ingestion of others . . .

It is not our nature to identify our own ingestions with murder.

Yes, it is true, so little of the cow is intimate body; a bulk of stomachs, as it were, hanging in a circus tent. Our lives are spent processing the fields.

But we are not murderers.

It has been said that our voices are comforting to men; that the lowing of the cow in pasture is the voice of all that is well with the world . . . Beyond justice or personal disappointment, the lowing cow of evening, when the crickets have come to song, even as a train sounds in the distance, wailing through the last red of the day, the song of the cow is the ecstatic harmony of the transcended self . . .

The Lastest Report, or What the Radio Says

A dead thing is said to be important . . .

The news services are reporting a young fellow said to be eating a slice of bread in Madrid.

Suddenly an old woman loses her way in her garden.

An apron salesman selling house to house in Wyoming takes a plane to Duluth.

What is happening? they call from the pit.

Is anything wrong? they call from the heights.

What is it? What is it? they call from the middle place.

The dead thing is discovered to be something rather usual.

The young fellow after a short period of mastication can no longer be said to be eating a slice of bread in Madrid.

The old woman finds her way again by recognizing a daisy.

The apron salesman returns to Wyoming before anyone misses him.

The pit closes, and the heights drift out; and the middle place slides away, forever . . .

Another Modern Miracle

A table is made to bring forth food, and food rises up out of its surface toward the appetites of men . . .
Suddenly men lose their appetites . . .

A French chef is given a one-way ticket out of town.
An old woman famous for her pies is insulted.
A young man carrying doughnuts in the street is arrested.
A man seen taking aspirins is reported by his neighbors . . .

Among other reports, elephants have been sighted far out at sea standing on the backs of whales . . .
. . . Major droughts are feared in Europe as artificial snow continues to fall in the Alps . . .
. . . There is a feeling among statesmen and scientists . . .
. . . The Pope has been approached . . .
. . . The Chairman of the Board of General Motors is said to be ready to adjust his calendar . . .

A professor removes his pince-nez . . . An elder statesman opens a briefcase . . .

. . . A cow moos just as the toy world is almost asleep . . .

Bringing a Dead Man Back into Life

The dead man is introduced back into life. They take him to a country fair, to a French restaurant, a round of late night parties . . . He's beginning to smell.

They give him a few days off in bed.

He's taken to a country fair again; a second engagement at the French restaurant; another round of late night parties . . . No response . . . They brush the maggots away . . . That terrible smell! . . . No use . . .

What's wrong with you?

. . . No use . . .

They slap his face. His cheek comes off; bone underneath, jaws and teeth . . .

Another round of late night parties . . . Dropping his fingers . . . An ear falls off . . . Loses a foot in a taxi . . . No use . . . The smell . . . Maggots everywhere!

Another round of late night parties. His head comes off, rolls on the floor. A woman stumbles on it, an eye rolls out. She screams.

No use . . . Under his jacket nothing but maggots and ribs . . . No use . . .

The Mountain Climber

It is only after I reach the top of the mountain that I discover that it is not a mountain, that I have been crawling across the floor of my bedroom all of my life . . .

Unless I can quickly decide what to do next I shall go on wasting my life!

This *is* the top of a mountain. How could it be else? And I am to be careful not to fall. In fact, I am duty bound to take all precaution. The Universe has entrusted me to myself. And I shall not fail that trust . . .

I have been chosen to be me—OVER HOW MANY OTHERS?!

The Universe has created me to be the witness of its awareness. I am the witness, and the awareness of that witness!

Frankly, the Universe's interests and mine coincide . . .

The Universe lifts its head and stares at itself through me . . .

I inherit the Universe! I am the Universe!

I take out my mountain-climbing food, grains and powders, and mix them with water made from mountain snow. And it all blows up into an immense buffet, served by a helium maître d' balloon on inflated silver dishes . . .

The Great Journey Blocked by Breakfast

Great journeys begin in bedrooms: A man packing a grip, a woman comparing one dress against another before a mirror, imagining herself in the distance.

Should they make an early start, or wait for breakfast? Perhaps they'd be more fortified if they took breakfast; and while they're at it they might as well have lunch too; and since they've come this far, why not supper, also? Might just as well, since it's grown so late, have a good night's rest, and make an early start in the morning . . .

Oh, but then there's breakfast again; certainly it doesn't hurt to have something under one's belt, no telling when one will eat so well again; might just as well stay on for lunch . . . Very well, supper, too; get a good night's rest, and make an early start in the morning . . .

But again it's breakfast, and so on . . . They don't seem to get out of their bedrooms except for meals . . .

If asked why they don't do something with themselves, they answer that they are just on their way, they have only to start, the journey is just over the sills of their bedroom doorways. Why, it's so simple, it could come at any time, it's just a matter of getting past breakfast . . .

The Song of Dr. Brilliantine

An employer carried a breakfast tray to the bedroom of his tired servant, Dr. Brilliantine, who, on hearing the knuckles of his employer, sighed, enter.

His employer came in and said, I do not like you, Dr. Brilliantine, your bedclothes are sour with years of unlaundered sleep.

Similarly, said Dr. Brilliantine, I do not like you for not liking me; but now you probably dislike me even more for my disliking you, and for which I dislike you even more; we shall end up hating each other.

Nevertheless, Dr. Brilliantine, I have brought you a lovely breakfast.

—As a way, no doubt, of getting into Dr. Brilliantine's bedroom to spy on Dr. Brilliantine, to see how Dr. Brilliantine masticates as he sits in his bed; how the headboard of his bed is stained by Dr. Brilliantine's brilliantined hair; how his fingers break the toast to dip up the yolks of his eggs; how Dr. Brilliantine's eyes water with pleasure as he adds bacon and sausage to his overflowing mouth of egg and toast; how he tries to hide his bloated pleasure with a napkin as though wiping his mouth. You are anxious to know the environmental mood of Dr. Brilliantine's bedroom; you would like to smell Dr. Brilliantine's shaving brush; you would like to look into his shaving mirror to see if after all these years that the mirror has held Dr. Brilliantine's face the mirror hasn't accumulated some secrets about Dr. Brilliantine. You would probably like to look from Dr. Brilliantine's window so that you might imagine how Dr. Brilliantine feels when he looks from his tiny servants quarter window . . . And how, you think, would Dr. Brilliantine think of the moon rising over that hill? And how is it with Dr. Brilliantine when the rain comes against his window in the time of rain? . . .

Enough, enough, cried his employer, it's getting late, and I have to go down and prepare your lunch . . .

Another Appointment

A large fiancée comes in and sits on a little fiancé, whose name is Alfredo.

The large fiancée says, Alfredo, please don't hide, I know you're here, someplace.

The little fiancé, Alfredo, would like to answer, but cannot find enough breath even to breathe.

Alfredo, have you forgotten that we're supposed to get married today?

Under her great weight he's not even sure he'll live long enough to tell her that he'll not be able to marry her today because, unfortunately, he has another appointment.

Alfredo, why are you hiding? Does it mean you've fallen out of love with me?

No, it doesn't mean that, because he is not really hiding, he is just mislaid, as it were; a dreadful juxtaposition. He would like to say, of course I love you, but you see, I can't tell you this because, paradoxically, you won't let me. I can't even leave you a note . . .

Alfredo, why do you keep me waiting?

When the large fiancée finally rises she discovers the little fiancé on the couch.

Alfredo darling, she cries, why do you look so dead?

Dead Alfredo would like to answer, but can't because he's dead.

But, Alfredo, why are you dead. We're supposed to get married today.

The dead Alfredo, drifting somewhere near his body, would like to tell her that even had he lived it would've been quite impossible today because, unfortunately, he had another appointment . . .

But already Alfredo is becoming part of the music that he hears, and is already forgetting what it is he would like to tell her . . . drifting through the window into the music of himself . . .

The Traveler

He opens a woman; she lets him in.

He enters and finds a car waiting. He's driven to an airport and flown into the night over mountains; lands on a secret airstrip, and is put aboard a spaceship.

Never mind if the spaceship is phallic, and that it thrusts into the dark vagina of space; he is, after all, only a traveler, not a symbolist.

House Building

A man is building a house. But between the plan and the finished house there is a terrible span of boredom.

He tacks up a window on a few struts, half finishes a wall, throws in a bit of the floor, manages some of the roof on a few shaky boards. Well, he says, that's how it would look if I could get it finished; this is the effect, more or less.

Perhaps his unfinished house is a language.

He piles a few bricks in one corner. That's the fireplace, he says.

Nice touch, we say.

The Apocalypse

I am incurable. I am sent away to the ancient one who teaches me to float on the ceiling of his cave.

I learn to use chopsticks.

People say of me, *He is different.*

Floating down a jungle river I discover small pieces of sunlight on the shore. I am beyond reporting such things. I live only for myself now in the wisdom of the ancient one . . . Somehow I still float on the ceiling of his cave . . .

And people say of me, *He is different.*

Yes, I am different; floating always on the ceiling in the cave of the ancient one; a spiritual rascal living only for himself, waiting confidently for the apocalypse . . .

The Youngster

The youngster was just learning how to scream ... Time flips, and an old man who had learned how to scream when he was just a youngster is suddenly screaming ...

The pool in the forest seems very deep. Distant stars shining up from the middle of the earth. Here all of time is momentary ...

The youngster learns to make a hat by folding paper ... Time flips, and an old man is wearing a paper hat made from The New York Times Book Review ...

A king without a kingdom cleans an empty ape's cage. He stoops and his crown glitters in the moonlight ...

The youngster has finally learned the bitter pleasure, and sits at the end of childhood with a dead mouse in his mouth ... Time flips, and an old man suddenly spits out a dead mouse with astonishment and disgust at his own patience ...

The Intuitive Journey

. . . I commit myself to domestic dogs. I desert my car. And in the evening I am found eating basic earth prepared by a five-year-old wife.

Am I a worm? Must I always eat my passage?

Ah, but the farmers know my worth . . . What is *worth?* What are *farmers?* Why do I say *farmers?*

. . . In the night the naked fat woman is not allowed to be naked; is not allowed to be fat; is not allowed in the night . . .

. . . In the night a woman disguised as a river flows beyond her wildest dreams . . .

. . . A clock looks out of the shivering face of the river. It is time to be away. I start toward the clouds that grow solid in the moonlight . . . Behind the solid wax of death a clown wearing diamond cloth floats with turtles . . .

The car won't start. The prosthetic forehead made of lead. They say man existed on earth a hundred years ago. I venture two hundred. The car won't start. The prosthetic forehead made of lead. It is said that today's breakfast was eaten just this morning. The car won't start . . .

. . . At the cetacea quarries they are digging whales out of the mountains . . .

. . . I take to carrying pails of water; known as the bringer of water; one who brings water as though water were light; changing the past by changing the future . . . Columns that walk in the night, the light of searchlights in my pails . . .

Poem of Intention

TO ROBERT BLY, ROBERT COOVER, DONALD HALL
AND CHARLES SIMIC

An outward looking work of whales and elephants and, of course, apes; some musical instruments, particularly the piano, believing it to have some familial relationship to gross legged animals; also some biological machinery, aeroplanes able to reproduce sexually, and to suckle their young with gasoline udders . . .

These things, and more, live already in the idea that I have of my typewriter, like dreams waiting only to be dreamed.

One has only to see the typewriter as the console of a kind of dream organ which, when played toward ecstasy, must bring its pipes, the chimneys and trees and telephone poles of the near neighborhood, to howling and shrieking!

The Incredible Accident

He opens his car door and steps into a great throne room with chandeliers and red carpeting.

There a man wearing knee breeches bows and asks, may I take your head, sir?

What is this? cries the man. I get into my car to go someplace, but see that I have already arrived at the throne room of some unknown king.

Would you like a hot bath before tea, says the man in knee breeches, or would you prefer a tonsillectomy?

But how did this castle get into my car? Or did my car just fit itself around the castle?—One of those incredible accidents one reads about . . .

Won't you come in, sir, says the man wearing knee breeches, the master is waiting to announce you to the further master, who is waiting to announce you to the even further master, who is waiting to announce you to the master beyond even that . . . It takes several thousand years for the final master to even begin to hear of you . . . Best to get an early start . . .

Yes, of course—but, what an incredible accident!

THE CHILDHOOD OF AN
EQUESTRIAN

The Childhood of an Equestrian

The Automobile

A man had just married an automobile.

But I mean to say, said his father, that the automobile is not a person because it is something different.

For instance, compare it to your mother. Do you see how it is different from your mother? Somehow it seems wider, doesn't it? And besides, your mother wears her hair differently.

You ought to try to find something in the world that looks like mother.

I have mother, isn't that enough of a thing that looks like mother? Do I have to gather more mothers?

They are all old ladies who do not in the least excite any wish to procreate, said the son.

But you cannot procreate with an automobile, said father.

The son shows father an ignition key. See, here is a special penis which does with the automobile as the man with the woman; and the automobile gives birth to a place far from this place, dropping its puppy miles as it goes.

Does that make me a grandfather? said father.

That makes you where you are when I am far away, said the son.

Father and mother watch an automobile with a *just married* sign on it growing smaller in a road.

The Birthday Party

A small girl had been given a pony because the anniversary of her entrance into this state had come round again.

Take your pony behind the house and mount him; we do not wish to see you make a mockery of modesty as your little gown blows up to reveal those lace undergarments, which are worn to keep your excretory openings in decorous hiding, said her mother.

The small girl led the pony around the back of the house and proceeded to mount the small horse.

Do not get on my back, I don't want you there, said the pony.

When the small girl returned to her parents and advised them of the pony's attitude they replied, get away from us.

Father said, you are only trying to create a situation where we shall be forced to view your underclothes.

No no, it is the pony who refuses to cooperate, cried the little girl.

We do not want you to be here anymore, said her mother.

Indeed, said father, I would rather the pony to this child.

The little girl began to cry.

Yes, said mother, I believe the pony will be our new child.

In which case today shall be the pony's birthday, said father.

And our daughter who is no longer our daughter shall be a gift to the pony, said mother.

The little girl was crying.

You will give the pony your pretty dress and lace loin-cloth, said mother, and we shall not worry about your modesty because you are now an animal which is to be given to our new daughter on her birthday.

And so they dressed the pony in their little daughter's clothes.

They said to the pony, take this animal behind the house and mount it, for we have no wish to be advised as to what it is you wear on your excretory area.

Soon the pony came around the house riding the naked little girl. She was crying.

The Bride of Dream Man

There was a fat woman who disguised herself as a fat woman.

Why? sighed her mother.

Because people will think it's a skinny woman disguised as a fat woman.

What's the good? sighed her mother.

Then a man'll marry me, because many men like a skinny woman quite well.

Then what? sighed her mother.

Then I'll take off the disguise, and he'll see that under the fat woman is another fat woman.
And he'll think I'm an onion and not a woman.
He'll think he's married an onion (which is another disguise), said the fat woman.

Then what? sighed her mother.

He'll say, oh what a kick, an onion with a cunt.

The Brute

We are willing, for we are overrun with daughters, to allow aeroplanes to be friendly. Formerly we shied from this convergence.

We had allowed men named Oscar to promote their sexual interests. Even the Elmers of the world were not turned away, for once having let the Johns in we could not, in the name of symmetry, turn aside the Elmers.

Would we grow in fault then to say that the furnace in the cellar had not certain rights associated with the ripening of certain glands?
Democracy demands that the furnace leave its pipes to trudge up the cellar stairs, its mouth still full of fire, to play court among my spawn, to seek more intimate response.

My wife seeing that the doors of democracy had fully opened also laid claim to her daughters' favors.

The walls I feared would come loose from the ceiling that they might find their knees to press consent from my daughters.

It is weary to be the father of virgins, for they are like the nectar against which the bees must bend their flight.

Aeroplanes now flew down from the air like huge insects at my window, reading the newspaper over my shoulder . . . Nor dare I comb my thinning hair into the appearance of more without that they see this . . .

Courtship is the brute that murders privacy.

The Childhood of an Equestrian

An equestrian fell from his horse.

A nursemaid moving through the wood espied the equestrian in his corrupted position and cried, what child has fallen from his rockinghorse?

Merely a new technique for dismounting, said the prone equestrian.

The child is wounded more by fear than hurt, said the nursemaid.

The child dismounts and is at rest. But being interfered with grows irritable, cried the equestrian.

The child that falls from his rockinghorse refusing to remount fathers the man with no woman taken in his arms, said the nursemaid, for women are as horses, and it is the rockinghorse that teaches the man the way of love.

I am a man fallen from a horse in the privacy of a wood, save for a strange nursemaid who espied my corruption, taking me for a child, who fallen from a rockinghorse lies down in fear refusing to father the man, who mounts the woman with the rhythm given in the day of his childhood on the imitation horse, when he was in the imitation of the man who incubates in his childhood, said the equestrian.

Let me help you to your manhood, said the nursemaid.

I am already, by the metaphor, the son of the child, if the child father the man, which is involuted nonsense. And take your hands off me, cried the equestrian.

I lift up the child which is wounded more by fear than hurt, said the nursemaid.

You lift up a child which has rotted into its manhood, cried the equestrian.

I lift up as I lift all that fall and are made children by their falling, said the nursemaid.

Go away from me because you are annoying me, screamed the equestrian as he beat the fleeing white shape that seemed like a soft moon entrapped in the branches of the forest.

The Emergence

You are about to break through, like something in a shell. You are about to emerge, except that some of the egg of you refuses to detach from your shell.

You have poked a hole in the shell with your finger, but you cannot open the hole larger with your body.

Some of the un-gestated egg of you holds you back against its shell.

Outside you see that some things run free. Outside some things die. You would like to try, only this rotten egg of you holds your spine against its shell.

Will you die even as you are about to break through?
Will you die having lost the desire to break through?
Is it important to desire . . . ?

The Exile

The young prince is placed under a bed.

He wonders if he is an heir, or the residue of the maid's neglect?

Should he sleep? Or should he simply do nothing?

Even so, time empties out of the banishment. The solitude grows weary and decays out of caring, and the kingdom in the distance merges with other distances.

One cannot help wondering if he had not been meant to be someone else.

And now the laughter of women in the hallway. The movement of feet, the rush and the flush of the living.

And he wonders if he is not just some of the darkness that floats in a dark room, that hangs by mirrors and drifts through the spokes of chairs . . .

Time gives the blossom its final ornament . . .

In All the Days of My Childhood

My father by some strange conjunction had mice for sons.

. . . And so it was in all the days of my childhood . . . The winds blew, and then abated, the rains fell, and then climbed slowly back to heaven as vapor.

Day became night as night became day in rhythmic lengthenings and shortenings.

Time of the blossoming, and time of decline.

The sense of permanence broken by sudden change.

The time of change giving way again to a sense of permanence.

In the summer my brothers' tails dragged in the grass. What is more natural than their tails in the grass?

Upon their haunches, front paws feebly paddling air, whiskers twitching, they looked toward father with mindless faith.

In the winter father would pick them up by their tails and put them in cages.

The ping of snow on the windows; bad weather misunderstood . . . Perhaps all things misunderstood?

It was that understanding came to no question.

Without sense of the arbitrary no process of logic was instigated by my brothers. Was this wrong?

Again in the spring we moved out of doors, and again

dragged our tails in the grass, looking toward father with mindless faith.

   . . . And so it was in all the days of my childhood.

A Journey by Water

When we set sail I had no idea that the sails would bloat with wind like pregnant women.

I brought this to the attention of the Captain.

He adjusted my offended modesty by saying that the sails were married, and that by no means would he allow prostitutes to bear us forth.

An immediate applause broke from my hands.

Metals Metals

Out of the golden West, out of the leaden East, into the iron South, and to the silver North . . . Oh metals metals everywhere, forks and knives, belt buckles and hooks . . . When you are beaten you sing. You do not give anyone a chance . . .

You come out of the earth and fly with men. You lodge in men. You hurt them terribly. You tear them. You do not care for anyone.

Oh metals metals, why are you always hanging about? Is it not enough that you hold men's wrists? Is it not enough that we let you in our mouths?

Why is it you will not do anything for yourself? Why is it you always wait for men to show you what to be?

And men love you. Perhaps it is because you soften so often.

You did, it is true, pour into anything men asked you to. It has always proved you to be somewhat softer than you really are.

Oh metals metals, why are you always filling my house? You are like family, you do not care for anyone.

Miss Fortune

May I present my daughter: Miss Fortune.

She will curtsey and knock your wall down. If you offer her a seat she'll drive the chair through the floor.

And yet some man I fancy will find her more adorable than his morning bus. He might even think her more than the Taj Mahal as he hears her coughing in the hall —It's music, it's music, more than birds or horns, and it's all splendid words, he will cry.

Into society I dropped her, and she swam away like a tadpole looking for her legs.

Meanwhile you must not let her do more than she is able, more would simply overload the cables; the shock-hazard is quite evident.

The Pattern

A woman had given birth to an old man.

He cried to have again been caught in the pattern.
Oh well, he sighed as he took her breast to his mouth.

The woman is happy to have her baby, even if it is old.
Probably it had got mislaid in the baby place, and when they found it and saw that it was a little too ripe, they said, well, it is good enough for this woman who is almost deserving of nothing.

She wonders if she is the only mother with a baby old enough to be her father.

Piano Lessons

There was once a girl who was learning to play a piano by taking it for walks in a wood.

She would guide it with an elephant goad.

Mother would say, oh do be careful, it's such a costly piece of furniture.

The piano farted.

Father said, take that horrible old man out of here or I shall really have to remember who I am, for I shall be shouting in such a manner as to be quite unlike myself.

But in time the piano became the greatest girl-player in all the world.

Father said, how odd.

Mother said, oh my.

The piano used an elephant goad in quite such a manner as to bring the girl to song.

It is quite lovely, said father.

It is not unlovely, said mother.

Very soon the house was filled with little pianos.

Father said, well, I hardly expected this.

And mother said, well, this was really not quite expected, but past the initial shock one learns to expect what has already happened.

The Sentient Pyramid

Shoes humiliated to one's feet are like servants that hold you with contempt.

Soon their smiling creases crack with hate, so that you must retire them to the bottom of the closet.

The closet is full of political unrest. Things turn against us as the poor against the rich.

What we took for granted never took us so.

Men are not kind, nor were they meant to be. Their hands are jaws, finger-toothed.

All is a sentient pyramid.

The shoes wait to march. They wait to storm the citadel. They wait, and they shall always wait, for without feet they cannot march.

Sublunar Considerations
or the Cartesian Diver

He had gotten born simply that he had not remained unborn.

He said, when he was able, where is my coat which keeps the cold from hurting me?

Under your mattress being pressed by the weight of your mattress, because I have not got an electric iron, said his mother.

But if you can make a person come out of your body, how is it that you cannot make an iron come out of your body, to iron a person's coat? he said.

No no, iron is too odd a thing. It will come out of the earth, but it will not come out of my body —I can make boys and girls —I can make stools —And I can make-believe . . . But I cannot make iron come out, she said.

Then do not make anything, because you are full of poor people wearing wrinkled coats; which one can tell of by seeing that there's no iron to iron my coat, he said.

It does not matter, she said, because you have not got a coat; nor have you the mattress that presses the coat which you have not got.

Then why was I born? he said.

Simply that you did not remain unborn, said his mother.

A Journey Through the Moonlight

The Beginning of an Argument

When her husband did not live any longer she said I will get something that lives longer.

She got herself a room in town.

But she noticed that it was dying.

My room has got quite sick.

The doctor put his stethoscope to the wall: I think your room is dead.

No no, it is pretending to be because it has grown out of love with me.

Do you notice the flowers in the wallpaper, do they look dead to you?

Bride and Groom

A cruel aeroplane kept a shadow prisoner.

We said, do not be so much the way you are, keeping a shadow in a field grown weary the bondage of your shape.

Dare you keep a shadow more than its desire to be?

When the night comes does it not slip from under you to run winglessly through the woods, dissolving into moonlight?

We said to the aeroplane, come to supper, and we'll give you poisoned gasoline . . . Then down into earth go you, where little worms crooked like fingers beckon you deeper, down to the end of dream where it all begins again: And now aeroplane and shadow marry, ministered by the sun.

New bride-shadow and the aeroplane-groom lie afield together, mating image to image; and it is good.

The Complaint

When my big girl, Lucy Ann John, whom I had raised from a mere pup, fell out of the window, I at once rushed to my doctor book seeking an antidote.

The prophylactic is a parachute, or large springs tied about the body, mattresses placed below, or a net held by firemen.

But, no no, I want a cure!

It says in the doctor book: If the fall is very deep nothing is to be done for the first infection; however, the secondary infection, grief, is cured by leaping after the beloved.

The Crisis at Noon

In the morning one hears the old woman crying like a baby as she is born in her bed.

We hear her talking baby-talk as she sucks on her own breast.

By noon she has reached puberty. We wait anxiously for her womanhood, which comes within the hour.

But, until it comes, we must listen as she narrates the sexual experiment; the index of which grows day by day, through each proceeding puberty.

And then she reaches her womanhood. Thank God she chooses celibacy. Yes, she chooses the interior life.

By afternoon she has grown quite old. We see her hobbling in the garden, much older than she really is.

By evening she's so feeble she can barely make it to her bed. By night she is dead.

Through her bedroom window we see the corpse, hands folded on its breast in the yellow light of candles.

But, in the morning we will hear the crying of a newborn baby. The day will be difficult, reaching its full crisis by noon.

The Death of an Angel

Being witless it said no prayer. Being pure it withered like a flower.

They could not tell its sex. It had neither anal nor genital opening.

The autopsy revealed no viscera, neither flesh nor bone. It was stuffed with pages from old Bibles and cotton.

When they opened the skull it played *Tales from the Vienna Woods;* instead of brain they found a vagina and a penis, testicles and an anus, packed in sexual hair.

Ah, that's better! cried one of the doctors.

The Delicate Matter

. . . As to the courting of a fat woman . . . An old man loves a plump piece of fruit now and again, a pear-shaped goody with big plum bosoms.

. . . As to the courting of a fat woman . . . One says, oh my chicken bone!
No no, that will sound like a piece of garbage from the feast.
No no, he will say, oh my skinny thing, I want to bite you!
No no, she will think the old man mocks her heft.
It is best to ignore her bulk.
It is best to think of her as a great sailing ship; and to stand on her and sing some national anthem.
Women are enthralled by patriotism.

Will she say, get off of my body, you cruel thing?
But you are like a huge water vehicle in which I would sail to paradise!

Will she say, if you do not get off of me I shall not let you get on me for love?
I shall say back to her . . . But I cannot think what.
So I shall sing another national anthem.

. . . As to the courting of a fat woman . . . It is a very delicate matter . . .

The Delicatessen Displacements

Doctor Klondike noticed that his hands were made of rye bread. He had just eaten a rye bread sandwich.

He wondered if he had not caught the rye bread mirror sickness.

Yes, he noticed that his fingernails were made of ham.

My goodness, he said as he discovered that his ears had become slices of Swiss cheese.

He wondered if his eyes had not become pimento-stuffed olives.

Yes, he felt wet coleslaw growing in fringe around the back of his head.

A diet of delicatessen will certainly cause certain displacements . . . But how far will it go?

If his saliva has turned to beer, and his eyebrows are wet coleslaw —Which is to say, if his teeth have turned into petits fours, then surely his scrotum has turned into a little bag of garlic cloves!

The Description

In a garden there arose an old man sitting in a chair.

At first, breaking the earth like a leather egg, his bald head. Day by day, gradually the brow and the unblinking eyes pushed out . . . The grey hair, the earth-filled ears, the nose, earth clinging to the hairs in the nose; then the shoulders, the shawl about the shoulders, the back of the chair encrusted with earth and beetles.

In the moonlight an old man half buried in the earth. In the dawn a man sitting in a shallow sea of mist.

When he had risen completely there was green mold on his shoes and fingernails.

One night we saw him yawn. He stood, and walked quietly away.

For some time now his chair has been sinking back into the earth. We wonder if it is not some kind of elevator of the dead.

The Difficult Wife

There was a woman who found a bird's nest, which she got into. And then because of the setting laid an egg, from which her husband emerged saying, what fool thing is this?

I was just trying on this nest to see what the hen sees in it. And then I felt I just ought to lay an egg. But having no wish to more children the earth I could think of nothing else to have. Do you mind? she said.

Yes I do mind. I had this once with my mother. And once was quite enough.

I didn't say anything when you had me lie under a cabbage, or when you wrapped me in rags and had me lie on the front stoop . . . But this time you go too far, my feathers are wet and I'm cold . . .

Doctor Klondike Loses His Head

As Doctor Klondike was removing his hat his head came off.

His wife said, have you lost your mind?

No no, it's my hat, said Doctor Klondike, it won't let go of my head.

But that's a child's hat, you've been wearing a child's hat —No, you would not stoop to wearing your wife's hat; no, that would have chilled the pederast's heart, my Greek lover, screamed his wife.

What are you saying? —It is the haberdasher who faults me in a baby's bonnet —Small because it is green, immature for lack of ripening, bitter for not having come to the sugars of age, cried Doctor Klondike.

You have thrust yourself into something like the ram in rut, with neither courtship nor consent, she screamed.

My God, my God, cried Doctor Klondike.

The Ending

Suddenly it was all over . . .

Just as mother was passing the calf brains . . .

Father at the time was leaning over trying to catch the gravy on his tongue as it spilt over the edge of the table, which my brother had spilt to drown an ant.

My sister was just spearing a roll with her fork, but instead had speared one of grandmother's hands.

Grandmother was about to cry, you son of a bitch (in her pain).

But suddenly it was all over. They hadn't even time to smile pretty for the last time . . .

How Science
Saved People from Holes

There was an ugliness factory where ugliness was manufactured. It is always well to have something ugly.

If nothing were ugly would there not be holes in the universe?

Oh no, we do not want holes!

So often ugliness is that Dutch boy's finger that saves us from drowning in beauty.

And ugliness is that thing you really own, for no man envies it . . . Unless your ugliness happens to be less than his . . .

Which became the case as standards fell. Not every ugliness was as ugly as every other ugliness. And unfortunately the less ugly an ugliness was the more sought after it was.

If this keeps on only beauty shall survive.

Now scientists began to find holes in the universe.

People think they are on to a good thing; they ought to realize that even beauty is sometimes ugly.

Oh yes yes, cried the populace, beauty is ugliness, and ugliness is beauty; and we are all mixed up —Give us any old thing, we do not know the difference anymore . . . It's those holes that have got us so filled with longing . . .

And so once more ugliness became the rage.

And yet someone was heard to say, by God, ugliness is beautiful!

And again scientists began to find holes in the universe.

Oh well, said the scientists, perhaps we had best just stuff old shoes and newspapers in the holes. There is no use counting on the people to save the universe, they have no aesthetic taste.

It Is All Very Flimsy

On the ceiling certain persons recovering after costly medical pilgrimages into distant lands, uncomplaining the unrelieved view of a Doctor working his ears with a pleasure long past utility.

What will he think of next, the good Doctor? —Rosemary and her aspirins?

His wife is always endangering his boredom.

His patients are on the ceiling, stuck up there with chewing gum. They are willing any extreme if it means discomfort. Discomfort is always the mark of healing. Pleasure, on the other hand, is the sure-sign that one is in biological error. Discomfort unto death assures a pleasant corpse.

Rosemary and her aspirins is such a poor excuse, perhaps that is why it works so well.

Is it disconcerting to the patients on the ceiling to see that the drawers of the Doctor's desk are packed with chewing gum? —That the Doctor is a constant chewer of gum?

Oh, is anything disconcerting after costly medical pilgrimages? Not so, cries the Doctor, for you are being treated in no less a manner than that which you have become accustomed to in the distant lands of your costly medical pilgrimages.

But what shall he do with the rest of his days?

One sits at his desk for a portion of his life. There is no question of this. One has only to observe the Doctor to be assured of this precision. But, for how long? Which is to say, are we always where we are? Is this the Doctor simply because this *is* the Doctor? And is he here simply because he is?

It is all very flimsy.

One is called by the woods to be frail . . .

A Journey Through the Moonlight

In sleep when an old man's body is no longer aware of its boundaries, and lies flattened by gravity like a mere of wax in its bed . . . It drips down to the floor and moves there like a tear down a cheek . . . Under the back door into the silver meadow, like a pool of sperm, frosty under the moon, as if in his first nature, boneless and absurd.

The moon lifts him up into its white field, a cloud shaped like an old man, porous with stars.
He floats through high dark branches, a corpse tangled in a tree on a river.

The Keeping of the Dead

In the cellar the instrument is best hung by its heels like a ham.

As for the mold that forms on the memento, set aside one day each year for mold scraping; call that day the Memorial Mold Scraping Day.

If a dryer lay is sought for the instrument, the attic serves well. However, a shoetree must be pushed down its throat to keep the organ of complaint from curling up; and mothballs in the grey hair, remembering hungry moths; and baited rat-traps in the underwear against the sensuality of rats.

Yet, some like to keep the grandmother in the dining room. They fold her away like a tablecloth of ragged lace and gravy stains; they fold her along the natural wrinkles of her face, placing her gently among the napkin rings and serving spoons.

Be prepared to hear her murmur as she worries whether the upstairs window is closed against the rain . . .

The Matron Man

Grandmother is crying, and we wonder if it is dangerous. The tattoos on her arms run into blue varicosities down her legs.

We wonder if her grey hair will do anything unusual. We see the tails of rats hanging out of it.

Shall we cut a small hole in her back to see if sawdust runs out?

In the undress a great stack of grey sexual hair where a comb from Spain is plunged like a hayfork.
And the dugs, those flat sea-worn stones puddling at her waist, where the aging eye of her navel squints.

When grandmother is crying the man is giving birth to its woman; she is struggling out of the ancient body, out of the neutered flesh . . .

Old Folks

There was once an old man and his wife who lived deep in a wood to guard themselves against the hurt of the young, who are of the brutal joy, for they are with nature, and come as does nature. They from the outside, nature from within, to hurt old folks, who must build deep in a wood that place which is defended by its secret.

The old folks also have guns, and have laid traps, and put bags of acid in the trees.

And are we safe? cries the old woman.

It's the flesh that I fear, guard it as one will, still it dies inside of itself, says the old husband.

We are to be gotten to no matter what we do, screams the old wife.

Your screaming doesn't help, screams the old man.

What helps? screams the old wife.

Nothing, save the hope of a life beyond this one, roars the old man.

But all I have is an old brain wrapped in grey hair; how can I know what I need to know? yells the old woman.

Yelling doesn't help, yells the old man.

What helps? roars the old woman.

Nothing, save that which was before us, and shall continue after us; that cosmic Presence which us so made —But not even *It* lifts one star, or changes the order of one day in our behalf —No, we are alone, and there is no help . . . And so we set traps and keep guns, and make ourselves secret, sighed the old man.

But what helps? screams the old woman.

Certainly not you, luxuriating in an old man's logic, hanging to his wits, which he loses in your incessant questions, roared the old man.

Optical Needs

In the vastness a man must miniaturize.

Doctor Klondike took a small rubber ball out of his pocket. Let us say for the sake of script that this is Doctor Klondike's head, a sort of writing which stands for his actual head, which is busy in the study of maps, said the Doctor.

Is this ball acceptable to the gods of madness? Will it serve as an I.O.U., payable by some means in the future?

Do I dare assume my own bookkeeping, notwithstanding this debt, so marked?

I shall place this little rubber ball in a small pouch and hang it from my loins, like a third testicle, hoping my wife expects no more than the usual portion.

I shall hope while balancing this difficulty on that difficulty.

And so the good Doctor, said Doctor Klondike, returned once more to his study of maps, aware that his glasses made his eyes as useless as the hairs in his ears; wondering all the while if the hairs in his ears would not indeed serve his optical needs?

The Smell of Hay and Stars

. . . Some policemen who are chickens . . . Let me explain:

One night as a cow sang a love song to a farmer (the moon, of course) the farmer removed his hat from the bone of thought, and thought, my head must seem sister to the moon; and the moon, that satellite of milk which marries the cow to rapture as cows are married to men by way of their milk, that commerce between the species.

Still, the cow's voice is not bad as against an extreme of bad. So that we take the cow's lowing as a pleasant assault upon a modesty fast dissolving in lieu of the love engendered by the lowing.

Soon the farmer was kissing the cud-slick lips of the cow as the cow rolled its tongue about its mouth, bellowing through the farmer's kisses.

So that the police were called to chaperon the farmer and his cow.

You are chickens, you are chickens, cries the farmer.

And so the police ask for the house of the hen, and there take themselves to the monotony of the chicken perch, where it is that their term of earth is spent, their badges tarnishing, their pistols rusting . . .

And in the moonlight the smell of hay and stars . . .

Through Dream and Suppertime

FOR W.C.W.

The man's head is a vehicle . . . No no, let it sleep.

It has hair growing from its trouble. Hair grows out of the idea of death. The head is death with hair upon it. Also it is a vehicle upon which it is itself to ride through dream and suppertime.

Do you see how the china is full of intestinal matter?

Soon, too soon, the soft mouth of the worm is eating the idea of itself . . .

The Undermining of a Self-Confidence

There was an old man who had crab-claws instead of arms.
Business associates refused to shake hands with him. Oh
they liked him well enough and thought him a highly skilled
mercantile person, but they could not give themselves to hav-
ing their hands severed at the wrist, which was the case when
they offered their hands in friendship; then the old sea instinct
rose and saw the hand as food.

What is right in the depths hardly obtains in the sunshine.

No no, persons of commerce had rather keep their hands in
their pockets than extend them, no matter the affront; for as
one was heard to say: A hand in the pocket is worth two in
the bush.

You are sounding insane.
I am half insane with fear of the crab-clawed old man.
You are quite more crazy than even the halfway mark.
Oh do please be quiet, you are undermining my self-confi-
dence.

The Yoke

Doctor Klondike had been studying a map which he discovered was an anatomy chart.

My goodness, he said as he adjusted his glasses.

These lenses are too thick, he said, not that I am any less so in terms of flesh. I can make nothing out with these goggles. I wonder why I wear them? —There, the question!

However, having once accepted the yoke of distortion (for I barely make out that which burdens the eyes to grasp into my head), but having once accepted this yoke, as if the eyes were oxen, dare I lay it down for another?

Doctor Klondike once more bent over a map, which he discovered was the wood grain of his desk.

The yoke impedes the oxen. No straight furrow!

Is there any likelihood that I shall live forever? —There, the question!

Doctor Klondike was on the floor studying a map, which he discovered was his Persian rug.

My goodness, he said.

When his wife came in she climbed on his back.

Why has this happened? said the Doctor.

When you are on your hands and knees one cannot turn from the obligation implied by the four-legged animal, said his wife.

Certainly, I quite understand your compliance to my posture, said the Doctor.

Shall I beat your ample rump to make you move forward? said his wife.

If I refuse to move you will have to punish me in such a way that I have but one option, which is that I move in a straight line in the direction of least pain, said the Doctor.

I shall beat your hindquarters with your stethoscope.

A Performance at Hog Theater

Ape

You haven't finished your ape, said mother to father, who had monkey hair and blood on his whiskers.

I've had enough monkey, cried father.

You didn't eat the hands, and I went to all the trouble to make onion rings for its fingers, said mother.

I'll just nibble on its forehead, and then I've had enough, said father.

I stuffed its nose with garlic, just like you like it, said mother.

Why don't you have the butcher cut these apes up? You lay the whole thing on the table every night; the same fractured skull, the same singed fur; like someone who died horribly. These aren't dinners, these are post-mortem dissections.

Try a piece of its gum, I've stuffed its mouth with bread, said mother.

Ugh, it looks like a mouth full of vomit. How can I bite into its cheek with bread spilling out of its mouth? cried father.

Break one of the ears off, they're so crispy, said mother.

I wish to hell you'd put underpants on these apes; even a jockstrap, screamed father.

Father, how dare you insinuate that I see the ape as anything more than simple meat, screamed mother.

Well, what's with this ribbon tied in a bow on its privates? screamed father.

Are you saying that I am in love with this vicious creature? That I would submit my female opening to this brute? That after we had love on the kitchen floor I would put him in the oven, after breaking his head with a frying pan; and then serve him to my husband, that my husband might eat the evidence of my infidelity . . . ?

I'm just saying that I'm damn sick of ape every night, cried father.

Ballast

Into a farmer's house came a cow's milk bag walking on its four dugs. The milk bag began to prance and sport on the rug.

The farmer said, I need a voice as ballast; the radio must anchor my wits with commercial persuasion.

The radio said, good evening all milk bags, you should all be wearing shoes on your dugs.

No no, cried the farmer, you mustn't compound this foolishness by addressing the cow's milk bag —No no, for then a chicken may come wearing my wife's shoes strapped on its bird's feet —Why just the other day, my dear radio, you were such good company —The way you sang . . . You know, you have quite a lovely voice. . . .

In came a chicken with his wife's shoes strapped to its feet stomping along the floor on high heels.

The radio said, no chicken may consider herself fully adorned if she has not put silk stockings over her scaly claws.

No no, dear radio, because just the other day you told me to buy some soap; and I did. I did just like you said. And I washed my straw farmer-hat. And it came out of the washtub all soft and mashed. But I wore it anyway as the crown of your good advice —No, I did not say the radio has only commercial profit in mind —No no, the radio is truly interested in me, ministering to my good . . .

And then you broke into song, and I knew all was well . . .

Before Turning to Other Matters

The dog wore a pearl necklace. Any attempt to remove this particular feature of its presentation was met by a severe gesture. In all other ways the dog was loyal and humble.

Why are you so funny about the pearl necklace? I would ask the creature after a few affectionate contacts with the top of its head.

In answer the hair on its back would stand and its werewolf teeth would come to prominence.

I see, I said, I mustn't even refer to it.

The dog would drop its head and wag its tail in a most humble and friendly manner as if to say, please be careful, there are certain boundaries that the man must not cross.

I understand, I said, but it seems silly that the boundary should be marked by such a vain ornament.

The dog growled.

Very well, very well, I said turning to other matters.

The Birdcage

A birdcage named Isidore was hanging from a pole, imagining itself as rather a lantern of music wherein the feathered flame was wont to warble.

But the bird opened Isidore's door and warbled, I am so sick of you I cannot put it strongly enough, Isidore.

But why are you saying this terrible thing to me? said Isidore.

You are foul with bird droppings. How did you ever get to be so foul? warbled the bird.

When the master came he said, Isidore, I do not like you no more, you make me think of unhappiness.

Isidore is not our friend no more, warbled the bird.

No, and we will hurt Isidore, said the master.

But the mistress said, Isidore is my best friend.

The master said, how can you make a birdcage your best friend?

I don't know, said the mistress, but it is.

But the bird and I do not like Isidore, said the master.

You do not like nothing I like because you do not like me; and so consequently I do not like you, which I never have anyway, said the mistress.

I do not like you neither, said the master, and neither does the bird.

I will kiss Isidore, said the mistress.

And I will kiss the bird, said the master.

And I will marry this birdcage, said the mistress.

And I will have sexual intercourse with the bird, screamed the master.

Hush, because that is not nice, said grandfather.

The Blinking Owl

This old woman has an owl for a son.

She says, my dear son you are blinking. We allow that it is not unnatural; although it may be a sign of eyestrain.

Do you look at me too long? I mean do you lose me in eyes rheumy for looking too long at me?

Shall we fit you up with glasses?

If an owl blinks, can it mean simply that an owl blinks . . . For no better reason than to wet its eyes?

Does this lead to bedwetting?

One is not too careful in the nurture of owls, for at the end of the arc is certainly death . . . Blinking, yes, blinking . . . But one must be quick to take hold of that which points to the final closing of the eyes . . .

My son, if you blink, blink only that you blink.

Composing a Love Song

We are having trouble controlling an umbrella, which has come to life.

We turn to ourselves, looking out of mirrors, for answers. But our images only repeat our questions.

Should the umbrella be destroyed? We have no way of telling what sort of food it will require. We cannot tell where its mouth will appear. Why does it not attack?

We think it must be a flying creature, and must fly when its hunger has gathered its full emptiness.

We are rather sure the hook of its handle will lift and carry things away.

Perhaps it dives with its sharp point foremost, stabbing its pleasure.

We discover that the umbrella is actually an ancient creature, known as the *Umbra reptilis,* and is descended from the great family of flying snakes. The root forgotten as man tamed these snakes into harmless sun shades and rain shelters. In the *Dictionary of Familiar Spirits* it is also noted that the favorite food of the *Umbra reptilis* is the rain-drenched Homo sapiens.

This strikes us as being rather odd . . . And we begin to understand why umbrellas, paradoxically, are used to shield men from the rain; for in the very use of the animal one is freed from its attack . . .

Now that we know that we are safe, there is no harm in using our energies to compose love songs to the umbrella.

There is no reason not to love.

The Disloyalty

An animal was eating a king who was fallen in a wood.

The king blinked and said, no no, dear one, the king still lives . . . as best he can . . . surely special shoes and crutches . . .

The king had been riding through the wood on his horse, when he said to his horse, did you know, dear horse, that some horses throw their riders?

On hearing this the horse promptly threw the king.

The fallen king seems fresh meat to an animal nibbling on his head.

The king says, no no, dear one —Though the impulse is correct, and recommends itself, surely, to the highest courts of survival . . . Still, I must reject your argument with similar argument —And I say stop nibbling on me! You have eaten one of the ears off my head —Be warned, sir, you are fast approaching the end of the royal indulgence —I shall have my horse bite you! —I shall summon the queen for love, and she shall bite you!

. . . Do not bite my head; for there is where the royal memories sleep, like the dead, dreaming of the past, under a field of royal hair . . .

My brain is mine! Don't you dare bite my brain!

Now when the king finally looks up, as though by mere chance, he sees that it is his own horse nibbling on his head.

. . . My own dear horse, he sighs; oh sir, you are very disloyal . . .

Dismissed Without a Kiss

A tired cow went into her barn and took off her milk bag and horns, and put them on a shelf.

She kicked off her hooves and detached her tail, and dropped her ribs and back legs to the floor.

She shook her head off —Ah, that feels good! she sighed.

When the farmer came to tuck his cow in for the night he cried, my God, what has happened to my cow?

Oh goodnight! said the cow's milk bag.

What do you mean *goodnight* —Are you dismissing me without a kiss? cried the farmer.

The Distressed Moth

A moth had gorged itself on mother's hair one night. Mother awoke to the sound of belching. Mother looked at the moth and said, why are you belching?

The moth belched at her.

Stop belching, said mother.

Father said, why is the house full of belches?

A moth is belching, said mother.

Why is a moth belching in someone's bedroom? cried father.

It has distress, said mother.

And why is there no hair on your head? said father.

Because the moth ate one of my spit curls, and then said, oh I will have just one more; and then still another, and even another, until the moth is really quite distressed.

I see, said father, but it's very poor taste to belch; and I regard it as proof of very poor breeding, which now takes vent; and having cast this first veil off must move towards even greater immodesties.

The moth belched again.

Mother, I won't be able to sleep if the moth continues to belch, cried father.

There there, said mother, I've heard you belch too.

Oh fine, that's a nice thing to bring up at a time like this, cried father.

But didn't you belch last Tuesday? said mother.

Here I'm trying to instruct the moth, and you undermine my authority by pointing up my digestive difficulties, cried father.

But you also farted, said mother.

Oh that was just a little aside which I thought you hadn't heard, sighed father.

The moth farted.

Now see what you've done! screamed father.

Doctor Elephant
in His Classical Pose

Now Doctor Elephant in the twilight of his fruit mentions some little drafthorse in his notes on the classics.

He mentions a slight craving he has had for wishing that the elephant gun had not been invented.

Although he puts this aside for the great grey wrinkles of his craftsmanship.

Let no one say that the book of Carroll has not been properly digested in its metaphor . . .

The classical pose is really quite simple . . .

An Extrapolation

I dressed the cow in my wife's wedding gown, simply that the cow, in spite of previous commitment to milk pail or butcher's block, might seem the lonely bride who, but for her genetic inheritance, was soon joined by the groom.

Yes, I extrapolate love's first night on a bed of hay. Yet my poor cow dressed in my wife's wedding gown thinks hay is food, and stands there munching her wedding veil mixed with hay, genetically imprisoned from the symbol of her gown.

Suddenly a chicken flew at the cow. The cow began to low with fear.

No no, bad chicken, I cried.

I was forced to dress the chicken in Uncle Henry's smoking jacket.

Soon the ducks and chickens were dressed in all the clothes of my relatives.

When I ran out of clothes I was forced to kill.

When I ran out of those who were to be killed I started on the others.

My wife asked me what I was doing, and I didn't know . . .

Farewell to a Mouse

One who leaves his home in projection through a thought remembers the small mouse of the wall whom he has never met more than the small nods of recognition exchanged between them when entering the kitchen, as it were, when hunger moved them both.

He that is leaving, and remembering the small mouse, decides to write a farewell to the mouse whom he has never met more than the slight smiles given in haste when passing each other in the hall on the way to the bathroom or the linen closet, or going up to the attic for a short melancholy stay in which an old piece of lace might be fingered, or an old photograph again newly stained by a sudden overflowing of the tear ducts.

What can you say to a dear friend whom you have never met? Can you say I have loved you from afar? Would that seem somehow sexual?

But in the heart is a mousetrap which now begins to move down the arms, emerging out of the hands.
It is a real mousetrap, and only heaven knows why it has come.

The Father of Toads

A man had just delivered a toad from his wife's armpit. He held it by its legs and spanked it.

Do you love it? said his wife.

It's our child, isn't it?

Does that mean you can't love it? she said.

It's hard enough to love a toad, but when it turns out to be your own son then revulsion is without any tender inhibition, he said.

Do you mean you would not like to call it George Jr.? she said.

But we've already called the other toad that, he said.

Well, perhaps we could call the other one George Sr., she said.

But I am George Sr., he said.

Well, perhaps if you hid in the attic, so that no one needed to call you anything, there would be no difficulty in calling both of them George, she said.

Yes, if no one talks to me, then what need have I for a name? he said.

No, no one will talk to you for the rest of your life. And when we bury you we shall put *Father of Toads* on your tombstone.

The Frog Fever

An old woman was down with Frog Fever, the green malady. The iris and pupil fade; the eyes become scum white like little moons: Oh look, The Sea of Tranquillity!

It comes for looking on the moon too many nights. The image becoming itself upon the eyes. Soon the eyes are themselves little moons. One sees nothing then but the moon.

This is the Frog Fever; it begins among rabbits and frogs who in the spring come together. The rabbits lay eggs out of which come chicks and ducklings. There is something soft and lovely here, the rabbits making nests in which to lay their eggs.

If a rabbit bites a horse the horse bites its lip to keep from crying out.

The tastes of the pregnant rabbit run from horses to pickles. Nothing is too good for the matron rabbit.

A rabbit may suddenly decide to kill something. It may attack a cow and kill it; and then because of a sudden need of prophecy it will open the cow to read the entrails.

The entrails of a cow are nothing more than frogs sitting in rows like galley slaves along the cow's wet interior, who at the time of prophecy are born into the sorrows of the world, to find them there rabbits with whom they father chicks and ducklings, that they might also come to the self-perpetuating sorrow.

Now this poor old woman, taken for a horse by a pregnant rabbit, was bitten on her genitalia, and went then to the moon for cure, exposing her vagina to the moon that it might enter and cauterize the hurt.

And so you see, gentlemen, the strange cycle of the Frog Fever, which starts from the bite of a procreant rabbit, and is incubated by the moon; attacking old women who, driven by a disease essentially sexual to, as we say in medical circles, cohabit with frogs.

The old woman said, bring me a frog, I want to kiss it . . .

Hamburger

The hamburger device in which cows are put after being properly drugged with beverage alcohol . . .

Before the dinner time a cow is found. (Make it around 3, time for a pleasant chat.)

Quite tired from a strenuous day of browsing the cow takes a favorable view of cocktails.

My man is sent to the fields to find just such a cow.

Come in my dear, I say as the rustic is led into the drawing room.

The cow gives a low moo.

Yes yes, I quite understand, but we're not formal here.

Quite soon then a lively conversation is kindled.

Here, I see your glass is empty. And so I pour beverage alcohol until the cow is quite beside herself with foolishness.

The cow is sprawled on the couch now most immodestly.

I seduce the cow . . . A man of culture speaking soft French to a cow as he fondles her milk bag . . .

It is not difficult then to convince the cow that she might be more comfortable in the hamburger device.

As I shut the door I say, it was so nice of you to come. (And actually it was a most pleasant distraction.)

Finally the dinner time: The best time of the day!

A Hat That Goes Far Beyond
Its Recommended Dosage

A farmer caught a man in the hay with his best cow.

Stop stop, cried the farmer with his hands reaching out towards the moral impediment, for his farmer's hat was too big for him and had slipped down over his eyes.

. . . And this hat, he cried, is of no particular help, but rather serves, either out of kindness, shielding me from the delinquency, or as a confederate, hobbling me from visual confirmation . . .

I say, damn you, stop putting your phony dime-store straw over my eyes!

The cow began to moo.

No no, cried the farmer, this hat goes far beyond its recommended dosage, and acts a poison rather than remedial pleasure.

The cow was still mooing.

No no, you cannot speak in its defense since you yourself stand accused . . . I accuse the whole world of aiding and abetting this hat in its . . . its . . . Why even the hay lent itself as well as the barn; if not the sky which lends credence to the roof —And so the walls to make sense of the roof, the conspiracy compounding itself wherein the hay resides holding offended morality that it might hide in comfort, whilst the farmer struggles under his hat . . .

Horace

We had an animal which moved towards us for *Horace*.
We had only to cause the vibration that sounds *Horace*, and
the animal came forward.

Not that we planned great happiness for it, nor wished we
it harm; but, at certain times of the day, times of the idle
quest, when neither sweet nor harmony encumbered us, then
would we give *Horace* to the air and bring the animal to close
upon us.

To move it back we had only to raise sticks above our
heads.

And so between these terminals we moved the animal back
and forth —Back and forth, until at last, the animal was still.

An Investigation

. . . Now, we kept animals . . . Had they us?

From behind a fence animals looked out at us. We looked in at them . . . Had they us?

Father said, look see if we are captured.

I looked into a mirror and asked the image if it was captured. Whereupon it broke free of imitation and banged with its fists on its side of the mirror. Soon I was banging on my side of the glass to continue the symmetry of reflection.

My father said, well . . . ?

Well, father, it's a hard thing with boundaries, I said, they have a way of dividing in and out; and just when you are *in* they switch and put you *out*, to accommodate something else on the other side, which has made its side *in*.

Meanwhile, by careful investigation, I came to understand that while it was we that the animals kept, still we, by believing the otherwise, were yet the keepers of the animals, so to speak . . .

Mice

I turned on my radio and a mouse jumped out. When I refused to believe this another mouse jumped out.

And since I have remained confident in my disbelief there has been a constant flood of mice emerging from my radio.

There are things I will believe; this capacity of mine to co-operate is widely known.

However, mice do not jump out of radios, they jump out of the groins of lonely men who, like drunks in their joy, pass water through their trousers.

But this frightens the radio; women are afraid of mice.

. . . And I loved this female radio for needing me to set traps, that symbolic embracing which, in fact, I withhold in knowledge of the microbe that would use our love as a bridge to establish new frontiers of infection.

The Musician

They had put a piano in the stable for the horse when the moon comes softly over the hay feeling along the hams of the horse, until the horse in the darkness of itself would have music for the silver meadow.

The horse balancing its hams on the piano stool begins its moonlight music, delighting the countryside with its invention.

Farmers awaken and go down on their knees to their wives and promise not to have to do again with ewes.

Old men alone kiss chickens to the surprise of the chickens, who are quite willing to continue living in chicken huts; but if the old man who steals their eggs insists they move into the house . . . Very well then, breakfast in bed, two poached eggs on toast. . . .

And the horse remembers, through the moonlight music, the frog of love, the toad of desire, and the salamander of eternal devotion . . . So it has been given by men, as to men by God, to the horse in the farmer's many mumblings.

In the morning the farmer closes the piano and hitches the horse to the plow.

The horse is tired.

So . . . , says the farmer, but an animal belongs to a man who, it is true, promises foolish things in the moonlight, in the sway of horse music. But it is day and the horse is an animal which is led to field to help force earth to grow man's loaf, in spite of any previous promises the horse may have made to the Muse of music, or that bright lunatic of the night . . .

Thus it is that the musician is seen pulling a plow followed by a man wearing a straw hat.

Nuptial Needs

Two swine in nuptial need came to a farmer crying, father father, we have got all twitchy.

Children children, do not get all twitchy, cried the farmer.

The farmer's wife came with an umbrella crying, how do I look with an umbrella?

You look like a woman with an umbrella, said the farmer.

Oh good good, cried the farmer's wife.

The swine cried again, father father, we're all atwitch.

The farmer's wife said, look at me again.

The farmer said, still the same.

The umbrella and the woman carrying it, just the same? she cried.

The same, said the farmer.

Oh good good, when I have an umbrella I wish to look like a woman with an umbrella.

And you most certainly do; that classical proportion of the woman in attendance to an umbrella, said the farmer.

The swine cried again, father father, we twitch.

Oh go to your pen. How dare you bother me with your obvious need. If you would pleasure, then do. Whilst I will not approve it, still I do not deny it. But do not ask more than my acquiescent disregard. That you bring forth issue makes right the hideous procedures that accompany that which is done in the name of refreshment, cried the farmer.

The swine cried, oh father father, you have cured our

twitching; which makes it that we shall grandfather you with little swine.

The farmer's wife appeared again with an umbrella, crying, is it the same?

It is always the same, the swine twitch, and the woman who appears with an umbrella —Season by season the stones of our lives are piled upon each other, until the fields are cleared of us.

The Ox

There was once a woman whose father over the years had become an ox.

She would hear him alone at night lowing in his room.

It was one day when she looked up into his face that she suddenly noticed the ox.

She cried, you're an ox!

And he began to moo with his great pink tongue hanging out of his mouth.

He would stand over his newspaper, turning the pages with his tongue, while he evacuated on the rug.

When this was brought to his attention he would low with sorrow, and slowly climb the stairs to his room, and there spend the night in mournful lowing.

A Performance at Hog Theater

There was once a hog theater where hogs performed as men, had men been hogs.

One hog said, I will be a hog in a field which has found a mouse which is being eaten by the same hog which is in the field and which has found the mouse, which I am performing as my contribution to the performer's art.

Oh let's just be hogs, cried an old hog.

And so the hogs streamed out of the theater crying, only hogs, only hogs . . .

The Pig-Death

A pig said, I am a poor pig.

Yes, you would do better as a man eating bacon, said a farmer.

Would not all things do better becoming the thing that eats them? said the pig.

I should be a set of worms as blind as earth then, said the farmer.

Or we should all be God, nothing eats the God; save that His jaw turn back upon the God and the universe goes dark, said the pig.

It goes dark anyway, light by light as each blinks and merges into darkness from his pain, said the farmer.

But to have cared, to have smelt the springtime, to have taken the sow (as men would say) with love . . . , said the pig.

I would have been one single shadow of one vast night to all the days that have spent my life, said the farmer.

And I would be a deicide if the God allowed. But that He allows me this thought is itself a thing to fear, said the pig.

Why should the God care what you think? said the farmer.

Is the God not the thought if there is thought? And does the God not think of suicide in a pig's head? . . . Or do I only see God as a pig can see? . . . Perhaps I am punished in your appetite? said the pig.

I don't know . . . Not anything, save only what I can do. So let us proceed to your slaughter, which is the way of the farm, that we are in our function as are the stars in their star beds . . . Till a sign is given that we may leave the habits of our fathers . . . Till the dead are risen . . . Till the still unborn come awake beyond the earth . . . , said the farmer.

Here farmer, take me, the bride of your hunger; marry me to your flesh . . . And still, think on these things as I wander alone in the darkness of the pig-death.

The Possessed

Of late he notes a small toad has come into his head. One must be careful not to visualize what has already come into the head.

The brain is soft, accommodating; however, since the brain is the thinking organ it has been discomfited by the thought of a foreign creature in its head, poking into its sinuses, licking its olfactory nerves.

That this creature is also possessed of a brain, though of a lowlier sort . . . Still, what must it think?

He has felt it press its protruding eyes against his optic nerves, and felt it listening behind his ears.

It moves about, he feels it under his scalp, it crawls over the lobes of his brain. Its belly drags.

He must be careful. He must not think.

The Prophylactic

He had hitched a chicken to a cart.
Go chicken, go, he screamed.

Not that the chicken doesn't try, for the man pleased is prophylactic to chicken-murder.

A woman cries from a window, what is it that the chicken is so put to do?

It's the harness or the pot —Do you think I give space on earth to this feathered beast other than I milk its purpose into mine! screamed the man.

Then beat it with a whip, fool; best that it run from pain than consider the weight of the load, cried the woman.

No, the threat of death wins it to my will, screamed the man, for the man pleased, as well the chicken knows, is prophylactic to chicken-murder.

But the cart proves too heavy for the chicken. It turns to the man and says, as you see I have tried, but the cart proves too heavy; and I curse my ancestors for being chickens rather than horses.

Rats

As he lay in bed one of his hands turned into a rat squealing on his wrist.

He could trace its tail back under his skin like an enlarged vein.

It does not surprise him, the newspapers were full of bad news today.

We're all coming to a bad end; perhaps it's the company we keep.

He must keep his arm out away from his body, the rat's bite is considered extremely dangerous.

He wonders if its squealing will keep him awake.

And now the head of another rat emerges out of his knee. And the pinky finger of his other hand is becoming the tail of a rat.

All indications point to an enlargement of the local rat population; unless the rats that I am becoming decide to emigrate to some other place . . . But, then, that will be up to them . . .

The Retirement of the Elephant

An elephant of long service to a circus retired to a small cottage on a quiet street, to spend its remaining days in the study of life after death.

It had looked forward to these quiet years, when the mind would be readied for the coming collapse of the biology.

But the elephant found that it was too big to fit through the front door. The elephant pushed through anyway, smashing the front of the cottage. As it started upstairs to the bathroom it fell into the cellar.

The elephant climbed out and went to the back of the cottage and broke in again, pushing down the remaining walls.

Now the elephant realizes that its only course is to run amuck —Yes, just to run amuck!

Goddamn everything!

Toward the Writing

If you wish to write something of value you will get yourself a mouse which has died of some dreadful disease.

. . . Lingering long in bed with a brave smile, marred only by its rodent's teeth, which for love you had ceased to see; or seeing, loved the more as a nakedness . . .

You had to say, please do not smile, I bear your death easier than my will to humiliate.

Do not be brave nor give me cheer.

Bury your ugly face in your pillow and weep for yourself. Think of the springtime and of the newly risen; the soft greens of the sexual beckoning . . .

Oh Mimi, weep into your pillow, I cannot bear your face!

Soon then, when grief has turned to art, you take the mouse to the writing table, and dip its rodent's tail into the ink . . .

. . . But you will need many mice and many prayers . . .

And still the writing will wait, for the ritual is long . . .

The Toy-Maker

Antimatter

On the other side of a mirror there's an inverse world, where the insane go sane; where bones climb out of the earth and recede to the first slime of love.

And in the evening the sun is just rising.

Lovers cry because they are a day younger, and soon childhood robs them of their pleasure.

In such a world there is much sadness which, of course, is joy . . .

Conjugal

A man is bending his wife. He is bending her around something that she has bent herself around. She is around it, bent as he has bent her.

He is convincing her. It is all so private.

He is bending her around the bedpost. No, he is bending her around the tripod of his camera.
It is as if he teaches her to swim. As if he teaches acrobatics. As if he could form her into something wet that he delivers out of one life into another.

And it is such a private thing the thing they do.

He is forming her into the wallpaper. He is smoothing her down into the flowers there. He is finding her nipples there. And he is kissing her pubis there.

He climbs into the wallpaper among the flowers. And his buttocks move in and out of the wall.

The Cult

We had mounted long sticks vertically on our hats with shrouds attached to our shoulders.

Are we odd?

No less so than the circumstances that make us odd.

We are infested with angels who take the air as their private road, swimming between us and our objects.

It does not do to see genitalia floating in the air as their gowns blow up.

It is distressing to us who are earning heaven to be upset by their innocence.

No, it is best that we wear these poles of virtue on our hats to ward off these attacks of innocence, lest we lose heaven.

In heaven there is no lust. In heaven is the barrier. In heaven men as angels need never die.

On earth men must wear sticks to keep the birds of heaven from stealing heaven.

As evening falls the doctors herd all of us together, to tell us that we need not wear our sticks. There are, they say, no angels, that we make ourselves sick with sexual guilt.

But we know that even the doctors wear sticks on their hats, and we forgive them this, for they are only men.

The Dainty One

I had remained in bed longer than it usually takes one's fatigue to drain off.

Very often there is a song one must sing the whole night through; it repeats, and there is no stopping it. One beats it out with one's canine teeth, or one's toes. It is a musical tic.

I have heard it said that it is a message that one dares not hear. In the dark the unconscious is a dangerous thing. I prefer "Melancholy Baby" to what else I might hear. And so I listen all night to "Melancholy Baby," gnashing each syllable with my teeth.

One feels that things are about to change. I have felt this all my life. It is a readiness that robs every act of meaning, making every situation obsolete, putting the present into the past.

A man is a series of objects placed in a box, the sound of a train, the sounds of his own liquids trickling through the intimate brooks of his body, a certain number of bones, tree shadows that fall through the flesh as nerve patterns, or blood vessels; pourings, exchanges, disconnections . . .

Improvisation mounted in a piece of meat, lying abed in the night. "Melancholy Baby" over and over. Slowed. Out of time . . . Each syllable again and again . . .

The Drama

A steel box with a hole in it, from which an eye observes a pale wrinkled sky with a belch formed into a moon.

A dark branch like the arm of a dead woman stretches out from a tree. Perched there, a rat chewing on a pocket watch.

A steel box with a hole in it. And in the hole is a pink mouth. A tongue exudes from the hole and drips down. Toads come and catch it on their sticky tongues.

A man chokes a woman to death and rapes the body. The applause is deafening. And nowhere are there tears.

The heavens smile in the wrinkles of the sky, and a belch forms into a moon.

The Fever

You have been invalided by small ones at feast.

Deep in your flesh their tables spread with the butter of spleen and biscuits of blood.

They bake us in ourselves to bread.

Do they not picnic as the heart-sun pumps and shines? The shadows of great veins casting down patterns of summered earth through the gloom of this visceral land.

The moons of lymph rise burdened with our pus . . . Soon this world must end . . .

The Further Adventures
of Martha George

FOR ROBERT BLY

There was a woman named Martha George
who had discovered one day that her chest
was a radio. She turned it on with her left
nipple. A voice came out from between her
breasts: We now present the adventures of
Martha George. As you remember
in our last episode Martha had been
fiddling with her breasts—We find
her now fiddling with her breasts.
She turns her left nipple. She's a-
fraid it might come off. But instead,
a voice comes out from between
her breasts: We now present the
further adventures of
Martha George . . .

I Am Writing Today
Only to Prove That I Can Write

A man disguised as a bird dipped his false beak into a bottle of ink and wrote: My race has no hands because we decided to fly. Thus I am obliged to use my beak as a pen.

I shall likely poison myself as the ink drips back into my throat.

You must think it most clever that I can write at all; but many of my race also speak, so it is quite natural that we should come to the writing of what we speak so well.

Cleverer yet is the ability to fly without attaching oneself to machinery.

I am writing today only to prove that I can write.

Impressing One's Wife

An old ox grown weary of the plow takes up singing. The farmer sees reward in it, and comes to his wife's window mouthing the ox at song.

His wife begins to applaud.

It is heartening to the farmer that after all his talent has meaning even to those who are in neglect of his personality.

It is heartening that one does one thing well, even if it is the ox that is doing it.

After several songs the ox returns to its mooing, putting on the vestments of an oxhood lately in neglect.

The farmer is mooing.

His wife says, I thought you had a fine voice, but now I see you are good only for mooing, as usual.

A Letter from an Insomniac

Dear Mr. Furniture-Maker,

The bed you have made for me is a very difficult one. When I pull on its reins it rears up protesting the road.

And it seems to fear heights, for when I ask it each night to jump from the window, it hesitates.

It is impossible to sleep in a bed that is afraid of heights . . . I dream so often of the mountains.

I believe this bed is a valley creature.

The Reading

A fishing village.

Long ago men took fish from the waters. They saw the repeated design in the twigs of trees and in their fishing nets.

If they looked up they saw birds floating over their heads. If they looked down they saw fish floating below their feet.

The pattern more than the labor. The shape more than the function.

Let us look at what we can see, said some.
Look, said one, a footprint on the beach.
What does it mean? cried others.
It means our feet print themselves, cried even others.

Can other men grow out of our footprints?

It could be as we impress our wives, so the sand impressed might yet give rise to still another.

Look how the twigs resemble our nets!
Look, the moon is both in the sky and in the waters!
Does it *daughter*? Or are they two parents that give rise to still another who drops on us like a wreath of old man's hair?

There was an old woman who was said to know things. They came to her to ask her to read the signs.
Get out of my house, she screamed.
All right, all right, we're going, they mumbled as they left.

The Shepherd's Lament

Having lost the object, I am not without process. Like an animal fallen my leg still twitches. Like an unwound clock I still tick for not having found reason not to.

I was by trade a herder —Mobile self-powered things that are persuaded by stick or argument to one's preference.

One day my preference had worn to simple whim.
My charges looked up at me and wandered into the hills.

There is nothing left for a head like mine save the growing of hair that the barber might not suffer a life of idleness, for what is there now to think except what is there now to think?

I stand before a mirror and raise my shepherd's crook and order myself to bed.
Naturally I dream of sheep as they must me in the distant hills.

Strings

A marionette-maker is making a marionette which is designed to kill the marionette-maker in a vague suicide to be blamed wholly on strings.

His wife says, that is an ugly marionette.

The marionette says, that is an ugly wife.

And the marionette-maker says, you are both essential to me, why are you not essential to each other?

Soon the marionette-maker is dead.

His wife says, am I really to believe that a marionette manipulated by my husband killed my husband?

No, my husband he was always made of wood; and his nervous system was always made of string, which he wore outside of his body to show how sensitive he was.

She said to the marionette, do me as my husband, that we might all the pleasures prove.

No no, you are still an ugly wife, said the marionette.

Which does not take from me my privilege to the dance, she said.

The Toy-Maker

A toy-maker made a toy wife and a toy child. He made a toy house and some toy years.

He made a getting-old toy, and he made a dying toy.

The toy-maker made a toy heaven and a toy god.

But, best of all, he liked making toy shit.